T0266921

Are We There Yet?

ARE WE THERE YET?

JEFF ALLEN

SALEM
BOOKS
an imprint of Regnery Publishing
Washington, D.C.

Salem Books™ is a trademark of Salem Communications Holding Corporation.
Regnery® and its colophon are registered trademarks of Salem Communications Holding Corporation.
Cataloging-in-Publication data on file with the Library of Congress.

ISBN: 978-1-68451-482-3
eISBN: 978-1-68451-503-5

Published in the United States by
Salem Books
An Imprint of Regnery Publishing
A Division of Salem Media Group
Washington, D.C.
www.SalemBooks.com

Manufactured in the United States of America

10 9 8 7 6 5 4 3 2 1

Books are available in quantity for promotional or premium use. For information on discounts and terms, please visit our website: www.SalemBooks.com.

I dedicate this book to all of those broken by addiction, past and present, who are on the road to recovery. The journey is long and one that should never be taken alone.

This book is also for the thousands of anonymous faces that helped me navigate my way to recovery. Every promise you made to me from that big blue book has come true.

CONTENTS

Foreword

Jeff and I have been friends for what most people would consider a long time. But I knew *of* Jeff Allen before we actually met.

At one point in my own life, I worked as a comic and enjoyed a degree of success, despite being aware that I was not "great." I came to that conclusion by honestly judging my material and delivery against that of the few comics I did consider worthy of that label.

For instance: Jerry Seinfeld was great. Louie Anderson was great. Steven Wright was great ten minutes at a time. Roseanne Barr had been great before she got a television show.

As you've probably gathered, "greatness" is more than a target. It was and still is a common topic of conversation among comics. "What constitutes greatness in a comedian?" we would ask. "Who, working right now, is on the verge of it? Who has the potential for greatness?"

There was one guy back in the '90s that everyone agreed was the full package. His material was a 10. His delivery was a 10. And his physical presence onstage—you couldn't take your eyes off the guy—was a 10. That one guy was Jeff Allen.

None of us knew him, but we'd seen the videos. He was sarcastic, biting, and brilliant. Comedians are not prone to laugh generously for each other, but we watched Jeff Allen and howled. His anger act was dead-on the best we'd ever seen. (It *was* an act, wasn't it?) The only thing none of us could ever figure out was why no one had stepped up to work with this guy in television or movies.

Several years later, I found out exactly why. And hang on—when you've read the first few chapters of this book, you'll understand why, too.

Fortunately for me, I met Jeff after THE significant change in his life so, while his comedy was as great as ever, Jeff Allen had become a different person. I met Tami at the same time, and I'm honored to say that the two of them are now significant influences in my life.

As you read *Are We There Yet?*, you will laugh, but consider yourself warned: you will also cringe during the book's first half. For the record, *Are We There Yet?* introduces us to four main characters. In the first eight chapters, we meet Jeff and Tami:

Jeff is an arrogant, self-centered, drug-using alcoholic who constantly ricochets between explosive anger and abject despair.

Tami is Jeff's wife and mother to their young children. No wilting flower, Tami gives as good as she gets. She is tough and caustic, despite being bewildered by Jeff's behavior, much of which has hurt her deeply.

It is not until the second half of the book that we are introduced to Jeff and Tami—a completely different couple who are similar to the first two in looks only.

Jeff is a humble man who cares deeply for his wife and children. He doesn't drink and, except for golf, isn't addicted to anything. Jeff is thoughtful, grateful, and optimistic.

Tami is Jeff's one true love, best friend, and partner in life. She is secure as a wife and mother; a friend to many and an example to many more. Tami is kind-hearted, beautiful . . . and may be funnier than her husband.

As I read *Are We There Yet?*, I couldn't help but create a list in my mind of the people to whom I will gift this amazing book. Not wanting to spoil the story for you, I purposefully left out any mention of what occurs in the time between the first Jeff and Tami and the second.

That is the part of the story that explains why Jeff is still alive, why Jeff and Tami are not only still married but happily so, and exactly what happened to create such dramatic changes in their lives.

And yes, you and I know people today who are much like the first Jeff and Tami were years ago. These are people who desperately need one of us to give them a copy of *Are We There Yet?* Personally, I will keep several on hand because this is a book that not only has the power to save marriages and families; it can also save lives.

Finally, I must say how honored I am to be called a friend of Jeff and Tami's. I am awed and inspired by their story and their willingness to share it with us. In addition, I must also add that at present, I am not alone in asserting that Jeff Allen is the most technically perfect stand-up comic working today.

His material is like music, his delivery is sharp and flawless . . . and his physical presence is hypnotic.

In this book, you'll find the secret to the joy-filled lives Jeff and Tami are now leading. Stay with the story as the scene is set in the first half so that you can fully appreciate the payoff in the second half. And as you read, know this: that very same payoff is available for you.

—**Andy Andrews**
New York Times bestselling author of *The Traveler's Gift* and *The Noticer*

CHAPTER 1

How Did We Get Here?

"So, do you want to get married?"

That was it. That was how I popped the question to the woman who would become my wife.

Not only did I overwhelm her with my words, I chose the most romantic setting imaginable to propose marriage: the airport baggage claim in Cleveland, Ohio. Right there amidst the blaring luggage arrival alarms, tumbling suitcases, and the occasional disembodied voice reminding me not to park in front of the terminal, I made my move.

And she could not have been more impressed.

"What?" she said.

I knew she was just blown away by my romantic technique, so I repeated the question to help her recover from her overwhelming surge of joy. I mean, what single mother of a two-year-old, greeting a comedian she had met at a performance just a few months earlier, wouldn't be overjoyed at the idea of marriage? After all, I had played dad for a week in Los Angeles since then and felt I could do this marriage-and-parenting thing. No problem.

"I love you, Tami, and I love Aaron. Do you want to get married?"

I inhaled confidently as I reached for my luggage, already a little concerned that she might not be able to contain her joy. I had decided I wanted to marry her on that flight from LA to Cleveland in between a nap and a bag of peanuts. (This was back in the 1980s, before everyone was allergic to everything.)

"You know . . . you and me." I wanted to clarify the situation in case she didn't know who the players were.

There I was, with no plan and no ring. (By the way, if you are a young single man reading this, for the love of God, have a plan and a ring.) I did smuggle a bag of peanuts off the plane, so in a pinch I thought I could offer her those instead of a ring, but I was pretty confident I wouldn't need to. (Obviously, romance courses through every vein in my body.)

I didn't know what to expect in the form of a response, never having asked anyone that question before. But I have seen movies—and Tami's reaction to my inquiry, I have to admit, was a tad perplexing.

"Yeah, I guess, if that's what you want."

That's what she said. Direct quote. And she said it so matter-of-factly, as if I had asked her if she wanted to eat breakfast at McDonald's. That's how excited she was at the prospect of spending the rest of her life with me.

You wanna get married and raise a family with me, until death do us part?

I guess, if that's what you want. No difference. OK, cool, I guess.

I gave her a hug and a kiss, and we were officially engaged. The luggage came and we headed out to McDonald's for breakfast. I can tell you this: Tami had no idea how much baggage she actually picked up that day. Turns out I was quite the catch!

Fast-forward eight years, and I found myself once again meeting her at a baggage claim. But this airport was in Phoenix, Arizona, and things felt really different.

As Tami walked toward me to retrieve her bags, there was no smile. Her face was red and her eyes were swollen. Tears left trails on her face; she wiped them away with one hand and reached for her luggage with the other. All I could do was put my arms around her and kiss her on the cheek.

"I'm sorry," I whispered. "We can get through this if we want."

"That's it?" she asked, tilting her face toward mine. I imagined we were attracting numerous looks from other passengers, but I didn't care. I avoided her gaze and reached for her suitcase.

"That's all I got left," I confessed. "I am exhausted, baby."

Two days earlier, I had dropped her off at that airport so she could "visit a friend in California." But when I awoke the next morning, something didn't feel right. On a whim, I called American Express and asked if my credit card was being used, and where.

That's how I found out my wife was in a hotel room somewhere in Southern California with another man. I actually called the room, and she answered the phone.

Tami and I had been planning to get a divorce for quite some time, but we had never gotten around to actually signing the papers. Instead, I had tossed them into a junk drawer, and we'd been sleeping in different rooms for most of the eighteen months since then.

So while I shouldn't have been totally shocked that this was the turn events had taken, I was. And I was livid.

Tami couldn't arrange a flight until 8:00 a.m. the next day, so I had twenty-four hours to marinate in my fury. Finally, after eight painful years of marriage in which I had felt like a complete failure, *she* was finally the bad guy! Had she come home that night, we would not be married today. I am sure of it.

Even though I had no relationship with God at the time, I believe it was His plan to visit me that night and take me through a long-overdue soul searching. Every time I thought, *How could she?!* another memory of a time I had shamed, humiliated, or treated Tami as inferior surfaced.

Remember the time in Boston when you did that . . . ?

Remember the time in New Jersey when you said this . . . ?

Remember the night in Phoenix when you didn't say what you knew you should have?

The more I remembered, the less angry I became. Try as I might to stay angry, I couldn't. It was odd, because anger was the one emotion I knew well. As Tami often said, anger was my "gift to the world." I had a close personal relationship with it.

But that night, I just couldn't stay angry. That night was a history lesson that taught me the kind of husband I had been to my wife. And it wasn't pretty.

As I lay there staring at the ceiling, slowly I stopped asking, *How could she?* and began realizing, *How could she not?*

So . . . Where Are We Going?

I've got to tell you: I really had no expectations of what marriage was going to be or what it even should be. I just figured that somehow, some way, everything would work out—roses and daises would always bloom around us, every dream would come true, and we would all live happily ever after. Again, I will repeat, I just wasn't clear on where, when, or how exactly that would happen.

Prior to getting married, I never thought about or planned anything, I did whatever my impulse drove me to do. It is a sad way to live, but if it's all you know, then it's how you exist. I certainly wasn't *living.* Someone once told me there is no smaller package than a man wrapped up in himself, and living to just feed all my compulsions made me about as small a man as I ever want to be.

Truthfully, if I thought at all about my future, it was only in terms of something that I would get to later. I always assumed that as I got older, I'd figure things out—that life would just sort of come together and the answers to the deep questions about meaning and purpose would somehow magically materialize for me.

All of it was supposed to arrive someday. But it seemed like *someday* kept getting stuck in traffic or something, because I found myself constantly looking around and asking, *Why am I not there yet?*

Maybe you've felt that way at times. Maybe you're a guy who set off on a career path thinking that if you just put in the time and sacrificed to climb the ladder of success, you would get "there." Truth be told, you thought you would have arrived somewhere or discovered something by now that would make it feel like life made sense—and yet here you are, feeling empty and unfulfilled. And you're angry about it.

Here's a question for you, one I challenge you to ask yourself and then listen for the answer at the gut level: How healthy is your marriage? I mean, how happy are *you* in your marriage? How happy is your spouse? I mean really, truly happy.

I ask because I know what it's like to begin marriage with the best intentions of loving someone until death do you part (I mean, who can top the baggage claim for romance?) and then grow more disconnected by the day. So maybe your marriage is struggling big time, even if you haven't brought yourself to admit it yet and no one else knows. But you know it's not good.

Maybe you've even begun to try to deaden the pain, numbing it with alcohol, drugs, porn, or other addictions that get you through the day. (Believe me, I've been there, done that.) You stumble through life, disenchanted with it all, but think that as long as you keep moving, no one will know how empty you feel inside, how meaning-less this thing called life really feels. It's not that you don't care about the people in your life. You do, but you wish you cared more and somehow didn't manage to hurt all of them so often when your deep-seated frustrations sneak out.

I know, I know. You're probably thinking, *You know, Jeff, for a comedian, this isn't a very funny book so far. I mean, aren't come-dians supposed to make us laugh so we can forget all our troubles?*

In a word, no. But I get what you're saying. That's what I used to think, too. *Just get people to laugh about this crappy experience called life, and it will help ease everyone's pain.* But that didn't work for me. After the laughter faded away, I didn't feel any better about my life. In fact, I felt worse. *Is this all there is? Just a few laughs and then we die?*

An Angry and Confused Piece of Play-Doh

That's where the anger came in. I desperately wanted there to *be* a "there" at which I could arrive someday, but I sure couldn't find it. Isn't that the promise of Wall Street? "Get this or that, and you will arrive." They never mention where that arrival is because they assume the consumer knows. Truth is, I had no clue; I just knew it wasn't where I was sitting at the moment. I was frustrated because I thought everyone else got it, just not me.

It made me become a person I didn't even like. Perhaps that is why, underneath the rhythms of life, there was always a deep under-current of anger within me, fueled by my frustrating and failing pursuit of something, anything, that would give my life meaning and purpose.

As I said, I'm a comedian by profession and have been performing on stages since 1978 in just about every setting imaginable. But to be candid, for many years my anger shaped my comedy. My gigs became an exercise in anger management—just without much management. For example, I would do bits on stage that were really just thinly veiled passive-aggressive attacks on my wife. All the other frustrated, hopeless men in the clubs would roar with laughter, but few others would—and Tami would leave in tears, asking why I hated her.

A fellow comedian once told me that the people who laugh the hardest at a show are the ones who most identify with you. They reflect who you are. Well, the people who came up to me after my shows for many years—the ones who told me they loved it—were angry men wearing wife-beaters who were either drunk or high. So what did that say about me?

When my friend told me that, I realized I needed to change—but I didn't. Or couldn't. Or so I thought.

No, instead, I did all sorts of stupid stuff, like getting so drunk I drove the wrong way on a Boston expressway in the early-morning hours and somehow made it home. Or the time I got busted for using cocaine right outside a comedy club after a performance. Or the time I got so angry I stood on a stool and screamed at Tami until she let me "win" the argument. Or, God help me, the time I got so angry I spanked my son—and scared myself in realizing the damage I was capable of inflicting.

And the list goes on . . . (I know what you're thinking: *How could his wife have stayed with him as long as she did?!*) Believe me, I hated every minute of the times I acted out that way. But I felt I couldn't help it. I didn't understand how to change. I just kept asking myself: *When will it get easier? When will I feel happy and fulfilled? Why am I not there yet?*

Here I was, someone who had made tens of thousands of people laugh on thousands of stages nationwide, but inside I was dying, my soul shriveling and hardening like a piece of Play-Doh left on the table of life. Over time, I guess I simply resigned myself to believing that there was no *there* there.

Until I had an encounter with the Living God.

The Burning Question

What I am about to share with you is my personal journey to find meaning and purpose in life. I'm not sharing it as a way of telling you what to do (or not do). And I'm not here to preach at you. Believe me, preaching is the last thing I wanted to hear when I was where you might be right now. Plus, I realize I don't know the details of your story, so I don't want to judge you or diagnose your situation.

And I've got to tell you, a lot of what I will share isn't pretty—but it is real and raw. I share it because I truly believe that hearing my story may help a lot of people who are feeling frustrated, empty, unfulfilled, and angry about it all.

So, if you are one of those people who feel like something important is missing from life, or you love someone who seems to have lost their way, I invite you to keep reading.

Here's why. As I hinted earlier, I am happily married right now to the same woman who sort of said yes at that baggage claim in Cleveland thirty-eight years ago. And we are not just *happily* married: our marriage is so much more than I could have hoped for. We're not perfect, not at all, but Tami and I love each other truly, madly, deeply. There is a saying in the twelve-step programs: "Don't give up before the miracle." Meaning it's coming, just hang in there. That is my invitation to you.

As for me, the anger and bitterness that defined so much of my life for so long is now gone. Oh, don't get me wrong. From time to time, I might get angry—that's just part of being human—but the lifestyle of rage and frequent outbursts of anger are gone. They've been replaced by a deep sense of peace, fulfillment, and yes, even joy.

How is that possible? you might ask. Well, that's what you'll discover in the pages to come.

But something pivotal did happen when I met my wife at that second baggage claim in Phoenix. In the twenty-four hours it took her to return home, I realized that I had become someone *I* didn't even like to live with—so how could I blame her for not wanting to be around me?

That's why all I could do was apologize. I really had nothing left to say. Not only was I physically exhausted, but I was emotionally destroyed as well. And I didn't have any answers.

The ride home from the airport that day was quiet, as many had been in the previous eight years of our life together. Finally, I broke the silence with the burning question:

How did we get here?

CHAPTER 2

Living an MIA Life

The more I tell my story, the more I realize my experience is not unique. So many men (and women) feel empty and unfulfilled. They reach a point where they thought they should feel fulfilled, accomplished, and like life has a deeper purpose—but they've still got nothing. Oh, they go through the motions, at least when other people are around, but behind closed doors and "in the windmills of their minds," the frustration deepens. They slowly begin feeling as if they've been swindled, bamboozled, sold a bill of goods—you get the idea. They feel certain that they should have reached their destination by now, but instead they lie in bed at night, staring into the darkness, wondering, *Are we there yet?* But there is no *there* there. They begin living missing-in-action lives, going through the motions but not really being present, as the frustration and anger grow—affecting their marriage, children, and everything around them.

At the core, I believe every person is looking for meaning. We all are born wanting to be happy. I mean, it's right there in the original founding declaration of America: "life, liberty, and the pursuit of happiness." That's really as far as most of us ever get in defining what we want out of life. "I just wanna be happy." The question then becomes: How do we define that? Is it the next (fill in the blank)? Does the blank ever get filled in, or are we destined to constantly chase the next thing, lying to ourselves that when we get it, we will be forever fulfilled? The questions and the answers are not unique to the individual; this is something we human beings all share. From where does that shared desire for happiness and fulfillment in life come? It's like we were made for something more than simply going through the motions and running out the clock in life.

Through many conversations over the years with other men who feel these frustrations, I've realized the journey to quiet despair often begins early in life. We may have dreams as children, but dysfunctional families can do them considerable damage. If we don't get connected with the cool crowd in the awkward middle school years, we try to survive and just make it to high school, where we'll constantly get peppered with the question, "What are you going to do with your life?" And the transition to adulthood is never as smooth as we think it should be. Truth be told, we just want to know who we are and where we belong, for somebody to tell us we've arrived. When none of this happens the way we thought it might, we can get pretty frustrated and even angry.

I know I did. I had barely hit my teens when I found a means of drowning the emptiness within myself so I could keep suppressing my angst and stumbling forward: alcohol.

Fatherly Influences

My family didn't seem that bad to me when I was growing up. My dad's father was a devout man of faith, and his younger brother was a pastor until he retired in his seventies from the Church of God. Both my grandfathers had passed away by the time I hit my teen years. But my father was completely different from his dad, and he had turned his back on his brother, the church, and God by the time I came along.

I didn't spend a lot of time with my father growing up, but as I got older, I realized he influenced me deeply. He was a large collective of contradictions. What he was able to do with his hands alone was amazing: he troweled concrete as well as he styled women's hair. He also painted some of the most beautiful portraits. As a matter of fact, one he painted of his jazz hero, Louis Armstrong, hangs in my living room today.

Dad was one of the best storytellers I have ever met. He could hold an entire party in the palm of his hand while he told the latest tale of all the "pudding brains and hunks of wood" he had encountered that week. People would roar with laughter listening to him. His ability to mimic dialects was uncanny—an ability I wish I had inherited from him, because it would have made what I do that much better. I did, however, inherit a love/hate for the game of golf from my father. I can honestly say that had it not been for our mutual love of this game, I don't think we would have spoken for over a decade.

Because there was also a dark side to Dad that was not pretty or fun to be around—much of which I unfortunately inherited as well.

My father was a screamer. He believed that everything bad that happened to him was an attempt by the Creator to ruin his life, from red lights to rainstorms. He claimed to be an atheist, but for someone who didn't believe in God, he certainly yelled in His direction a lot. His favorite thing to do was look at the heavens and scream, "Why me, Lord? Why is it always me?!" At first glance, one might think this to be a rhetorical question, but I honestly believed as I got older that he truly thought some invisible force in the universe was out to get him.

To this day, I have a negative script that plays in my head: *I'm a piece of crap.* I don't remember my father ever sitting me down and telling me that, but his verbal jabs and the comparisons to my older brother were constant. The reality was that if Dad was upset, which was often the case, everyone around him felt the brunt of it. He was an equal-opportunity frustration distributor.

It wasn't until decades later that I discovered his legacy of frustration began building before I was born. You see, my dad loved jazz music when he was younger. He played for a band in the U.S. Army—the 82nd Airborne Division Band, I believe. He played saxophone and clarinet; I was told he was invited to go to Juilliard in New York City. (He didn't talk about that; my aunt told me.) After he was discharged, he attended the University of Chicago fine arts program, painting portraits. But my mother's dad wouldn't let her marry an artist—so he got a "safe, reliable" construction job instead.

Over the years, he worked in concrete and masonry all over Chicago and took pride in what he produced. When I took my first real job in downtown Chicago, he would take me around and point out all the buildings he had worked on—most of which left a lot of his sweat and blood mixed in with the concrete. His claim to fame was that he had troweled the very last step on the highest point of the Sears Tower.

He took pride in his work, but his artistic heart wasn't in it. In fact, after we moved from Chicago to the suburb of Sauk Village when I was five years old, he would often hole up in his room for weeks every winter when the work slowed, only coming down to eat.

He did try other things to supplement his income. He got licensed to do women's hair, but that didn't last long. Women would come in with pictures of Elizabeth Taylor and say they wanted their hair cut like hers. Dad would decide those women could never look like Elizabeth, and cut their hair in the way he thought best. Apparently, there was no market for his way of doing things. I guess not one woman came in, sat down, and when asked how she wanted her hair styled, said, "Oh, surprise me, Jack!"

My mother got a job as well to supplement the family income, becoming one of the first women in our neighborhood to go to work full-time. But my father believed that a real man was the household breadwinner, so that fact cut him deeply. One night he lamented to me, "What kind of man has a wife who makes more money than he does?" It was a generational lament that cut deep.

The construction crowd taught my father to drink. By the time I was sentient, he was a functioning alcoholic. When he tried to quit, it only made things worse. One of his hard and fast rules was, "As long as I go to work and put a roof over your heads and food in your mouths, don't tell me what to do." After he missed a day of work because he couldn't get out of bed in the morning, he quit drinking for two years—but those two years were the most violent of his life because he didn't have alcohol to deaden his rage. He would lash out at all the inanimate objects that didn't cooperate with him. From automobile tires that went flat to televisions that wouldn't come in clear, he smashed them all.

One day, I came home from school and went into the bathroom—only to find there was no toilet seat, just a pile of ceramic powder on the floor where someone had beaten it to death. A few minutes later, Dad came home from the hardware store with a new toilet.

Whenever something didn't line up with my dad's expectations of how the world should be, he beat it—and that included his children. As the oldest, my brother usually received the brunt of our father's anger, nearly having his arm broken on more than one occasion. And like any good older brother, he passed the beatings along to me. I'd be sitting on the couch minding my own business, and he would attack me just for existing. He'd walk over, drag me off the couch, and just start pummeling me. He broke my nose twice. (That's how I got this lovely face.) My parents just said it was regular older-brother behavior, but I knew this was not normal; it was torture. He was five years older than me, so by the time I became a teenager, he had moved out of the house.

Growing up, I learned that whoever yells the loudest, smashes the most things, and is the most intimidating wins. Before my brother moved out, I was never the loudest or the biggest, so I generally just tried to run away or hide. Sometimes during those years, if I heard he was back in our neighborhood, I wouldn't sleep at home. He might come over, drag me out of bed, and beat me up for no reason.

Even so, I worshiped him as I was growing up. He was just the coolest. Like my dad in his early days, he was also a musician and a gifted writer. He wrote incredibly poetic songs and had an IQ around 140. More than one schoolteacher asked my parents what they could do to motivate my brother to write. But like my father, he started drinking at nineteen—and once he started, he never stopped. He checked into his first rehab in his early twenties. The doctors told my parents that he suffered from bipolar disorder, but he never would take any medication for it. Instead, he self-medicated with alcohol and even crack cocaine. (He lived on the streets off and on for years before passing away at age seventy-one from cirrhosis. Alcohol stole his entire youth, but I am proud to say that for the last six years of his life, he was sober.)

My mother was a saint. They were together and married for over fifty years, and her ability to let things roll off her back was nothing short of a miracle. She was the calm in the storm that was the men in her life, and she did it with a scorching dry sense of humor: "Oh, look, Jack, God made another light turn red."

I never understood why my mother stayed with my dad after we were all grown. Men from his generation were often conditioned not to show emotion or talk about their feelings. It wasn't until I got married and had my own issues to deal with that I began to understand that they had a deep love for each other that we weren't privy to.

It wasn't until near the end of his life, when my mom was dying of ovarian cancer, that I ever saw my father treat her in a caring way. He doted on her those last seven years like she was his heart and soul. It was amazing to watch; I'd like to think he did that a lot over the years when we weren't around. Mom deserved that.

After she passed, I thanked my dad for finally showing me the way a man should treat his wife. He said he didn't know what I was talking about.

Introducing . . . Alcohol!

Studies have found that alcoholics vividly remember their first drink. I was about thirteen when I had my first drink at my older sister's wedding—a seven and seven: 7UP mixed with Seagram's Seven Crown whiskey. I recall the warmth that washed over me.

It was an amazing feeling . . . until I woke up covered in my own vomit. There was no progression for me from social drinker to drunkard; right from the get-go, I drank until I threw up, and then I passed out. That behavior makes no sense. I mean, who would keep eating food that makes them puke every time they eat it? But I did. That's how smart I was.

My drinking habit took off from there. Every household had a liquor cabinet back then, and the drinking parties amongst the adults were frequent, so none of my friends' parents ever stopped us. We weren't even old enough to drive, but every week my buddies and I would get smashed. I'd be sick for five days with terrible hangovers.

And we weren't even good mixologists. One night, someone handed me a glass of orange juice with pulp and told me to fill the rest of it up with scotch. It tasted awful, but I drank it. It didn't take long for it to come back up. (That was the end of drinking orange juice for me. For a long time, I couldn't even bring it to my lips without convulsing. Why couldn't I have had that reaction to the alcohol instead?)

But I had learned from my dad that a real man can handle his liquor, so eventually my body learned to keep that down. Over time I developed a high tolerance and wore the fact that I could drink, drink, drink, and drink some more like a badge of pride. I felt I was finally a real man.

My older brother started to drink around the same time I did. Sometimes, I'd risk his wrath and go hang out at his place because he would buy me beer. My mother got suspicious because every time I came home from his place, I would have to pee three or four times in the middle of the night. I discovered I could just raise my bedroom window and urinate through that into the yard to keep her from finding me out. (That worked great until the morning the paperboy got an unwelcome shower.)

I chased that initial feeling from my first drink for years with alcohol and eventually other drugs. Consequently, I collected a handful of DUIs over the course of my late teen and young adult years. I ended up humiliated quite a few times as the town drunk. One night I passed out in the bar, only to wake up at closing time. When I stood up to leave, I fell flat on my face because while I was unconscious, the guys tied my shoes together. While I lay there humiliated, they were all laughing. I took one shoe off and walked home that way—limping, crying, and ashamed.

I first got the bug for performing in front of people when I was about sixteen. I once watched my older brother perform music in a club in Chicago, and a couple of comics opened for him. They were rocking the crowd, making people laugh, and I imagined they must have felt like the biggest guys in the room. I remember thinking, *I would love to do that.* But I had no idea *how* they did it. It's not like there is a stand-up-comedian booth on career day in high school, where they lay out the path to a successful career in comedy.

I had no idea how to start a career or pursue anything, really. I was directionless and drifting, using alcohol to drown the sense of emptiness within me, concealing it even from myself so I could keep moving forward from minute to minute, day to day. I had no plans, and that was just fine with me—until opportunities started passing me by.

One thing I was pretty good at during my teen years was baseball. Like millions of kids, I wanted to play professionally. When I was about fourteen years old, I was invited to play in an all-star tournament with teams from all over the state of Illinois. I had a great weekend and won the MVP award, one of the proudest moments of my young life.

Oddly, the conversation I had with my father the day I brought the trophy home wasn't a congratulatory one, but one on metaphysics. I was sitting on the couch admiring my trophy when Dad walked in and decided this was the moment to give me his thoughts on God and the universe.

"If one day you advance through the ranks and wind up playing professional baseball," he started, "someone's going to tell you those talents you have are God-given. When they do, you tell them to kiss your ass. There is no God." Then he went on a tirade about "God people" and their sophomoric view that God determines outcomes. "Those people" are never around for the hard work, he lamented; they see the finished product and just say, "Look what God did."

"God did nothing because there is no God," he said. "You are doing it all, Jeff." Sadly, I bought it all—hook, line, and sinker.

Decades later, someone told me that the word "inspiration" means "God breathed." That resonated with me because I really believe that God breathed into me a love for baseball—but as soon as I started telling people there was no God who gave me this talent, baseball became work. What gave me pure joy became a task and a chore. I truly believe that God did not take the talent from me; He just moved His breath on to someone else. The spark of inspiration was gone.

Then drinking moved to first place in my life—and that was that.

I found out years later how much my attitude destroyed opportunities. After I graduated from high school, a former team manager told me several Division I colleges had sent letters to my coach about me—but I never saw them because my coach threw them in the trash. He told those college coaches I was an insubordinate kid who wouldn't fit into their programs. And he was probably right. I know I didn't have the discipline on any level to work within a Division I system.

Instead, I attended a local community college on a baseball scholarship and hoped I could get drafted from there. I found out many years later that the Philadelphia Phillies had me on a short list of players they were tracking during my freshman year. They decided they would give me one more year to develop—and that was when my drinking finally pushed me off the team, out of baseball, and away from school. When the reality hit me that my baseball dream was finally dead, I mourned it like the loss of a good friend. It was a deep part of my soul that I simply threw away.

Missing Out for Drinking Up

Unfortunately, drinking wasn't exactly something I could get paid to do. Eventually, I had to get a job. But I had no idea what I wanted to do. I did construction for a summer with my brother and father. It was the most brutal summer of my young life; they mocked me mercilessly as I fell into the concrete repeatedly from exhaustion. That kind of work was not for me. To this day, I have nothing but a deep respect for the men and women who do it.

When I dropped out of college, the first question my dad asked, "School's over for you, what are you going to do for a living?" I told him the truth: I had no idea, but I was compiling a short list of things I was *not* going to do, and concrete was on the top of that list. I was not cut out for hard labor.

So I took a job at my uncle's jewelry company in Chicago and found my drinking crowd pretty quickly. One of my single friends bought a house that became the party palace. When he got engaged and moved in with his fiancée, his brother took over the house and continued the parties.

About that time, I got into cocaine. When my tolerance for alcohol decreased, I needed something to pick me back up. At first, I dabbled with coke, then I realized I could make money from it. So when someone offered the opportunity to become a dealer, I had nothing to hold me back. (Well, nothing except the fact that I was a terrible dealer.)

As a result of my poor selling skills and even worse work ethic, I found a guy to help me sell it. My supplier would give me an ounce of uncut Peruvian cocaine and tell me I owed him $2,200 at the end of the week. With twenty-eight grams to an ounce, if I sold a gram for $100, I could earn $2,800 without even diluting it. So I kept six grams for myself, gave my underling twenty-two grams, and told him I just wanted $2,200 back. He diluted it, adding fifteen grams of I don't even know what. So we all made money along the way.

Then about three weeks into our little arrangement, I went to a family reunion and was late making a payment. When I got home, I called my supplier to tell him I had his money.

"Get out of the house," he told me. "I got paper out on you."

"Okay . . . what's paper?" (Paper apparently is a contract that these guys use with other like-minded individuals to do their dirty work. It is all quite organized, know what I mean?)

"They're not going to kill you," he explained. "They're just going to break a couple of bones."

"Oh, that's good—I feel so much better . . . *What?* What are you talking about?"

"I'm sick of you guys," he snarled. "You're always late."

"What?" I really had no idea what he was talking about. "This is the first time!"

"Well, they're looking for you, so don't go to your usual places."

I snuck around town through back alleys until I finally found a way to get my supplier's money back to him without getting kneecapped.

"I'm out," I told him, almost throwing the money at him as I walked away.

"No, we're fine," he assured me, and offered me more cocaine.

"I'm not fine," I said, still shaking a bit from the close call.

My short-lived cocaine dealership ended just in time. I found out later from one of the cops in our town that I was on their radar. The word was out that I was dealing. "We just didn't know how much, you know," he told me.

The Funny Thing about Anger

I really believe God was in there somewhere. I had no awareness of it at the time, but I can just imagine God watching my scatter-brained decisions and saying to Himself, "Jeff, that's really stupid," and giving me a little flick with His finger.

Then, suddenly, I found the strength to just say no to all that stupidity. As I look back now, it was like He put up rails to keep me from completely going in the gutter. But I still had a lot of stupid left in me.

In August 1978, my coworkers at the jewelry store and I had just finished setting up for a show when they said they were going to a comedy club. I didn't know such things existed, but it caught my interest. After that, I was at the club every Tuesday, Thursday, and Sunday night—the open-mic nights—trying to work up the courage to go onstage.

Finally, on Thanksgiving night, I left my parents' house after dinner, drank enough liquid courage, and finally did it. Everybody who knew me came out to watch, so there were a lot of expectations when I finally stepped on stage. I don't remember anything except that it was horrific. I completely bombed, humiliated myself, crawled out of the club in shame, and sat in my car and cried.

Then I went home and punched a hole in my closet door. Then another one. That was my reaction to shame and humiliation—anger. What I realize now is that anger is usually a cover emotion for sadness.

Children tend to respond to hard stuff in life with a sense of resignation. After all, there often isn't much they can do. But there comes a moment when a child decides, "I'm not going to feel this anymore." And the sadness gets covered by anger. Then, every time sadness gets triggered, the body reacts with anger instead of resignation. The child lashes out—which is what I did that night and so many nights after that. I suppose it wasn't surprising; I had seen that behavior modeled my entire life, so I followed the same path without thinking about it.

But I still went back the very next open-mic night. I'm not sure if it was because I was a sadist or a masochist.

When I walked into the club, the emcee pulled me aside and said, "You're going to have to make some sense tonight. We're still trying to figure out what you said on Thursday."

And that was my start in comedy.

CHAPTER 3

Swipe Right for Rage

For some reason, even after such an illustrious initial showing, I kept doing comedy. Not because I had a great work ethic or some deep-seated desire to succeed in life; I have always said that if you like to nap, get a job in a mattress factory, and if you like to drink, get a job in a bar. I was always at the club, so I figured I might as well get paid for it.

It took six months for me to quit my job at the jewelry store. I had been making $300 a week there, but it was just too hard to party until two or three in the morning and then get up and go to work at 6:30. Something had to go, so rather than giving up drinking until the wee hours of the morning, I gave up the well-paying job to party and try to make people laugh.

Now I was living the dream—making $20 a week, sleeping on floors, and stealing pop bottles for the refunds so I could buy boxes of macaroni and cheese. I discovered how little I needed to live on when most everything I bought was either drunk or snorted. I also had terrible stage fright. There were nights that I would walk onto the stage, draw a blank, and leave. Emcees couldn't leave the room because they had no idea if I was going to last five minutes or five seconds. I thought I could make it in the comedy world—if only I could get over the nerves.

One club owner had a pay scale for comedians: $2.00, $5.00, $7.50, and $10.00 a show. I never made it to the $5.00 level. When he booted me out of the club one night, we got into an argument. "That's it," he said, "you're now a zero-dollar comic."

Not missing a beat, I brilliantly asked, "Which president is on *that* bill?"

He wasn't amused.

"This is how stupid you are," I told him, "You think I come here for the money? I drink forty dollars every night." It wasn't about the cash for me, only the drink.

Once, I quit drinking for six months. When I started up again, the owner told me he knew he could tell because he was running out of my brand of Miller Lite for the first time in six months.

Yes, I did try to quit drinking for a while around the time I turned twenty-five. I was having a hard time getting work, tired of just scraping by, and needed to make a change—so I went into an Air Force recruiter's office. The recruiter asked me why I wanted to join the military. "Why would anyone my age want to join the military?" I retorted. "I'm a loser." (Ever the comedian . . . but this guy didn't laugh.) "Look, I've got nothing," I said seriously. "I barely got through high school."

The military wasn't picky about my reasons for joining, and I had no legal issues on my record, so I took the written test and passed. Of course, I would never pass the *drug* test, but that didn't occur to me at the time.

I was scheduled to take the physical exam on a Wednesday, but an out-of-town comedy club friend called on Monday. "Somebody canceled," he said. "We need you here Tuesday night."

And that was it. Once I hooked up with that particular comedy club chain, then other clubs opened up. Soon my career as a comedian was off and running. And for some odd reason, the Air Force never called to try to get me back. It was as if they sensed my lack of discipline or something.

By the early 1980s, the country had exploded with comedy clubs, and the pool of comedians grew to match it. All the big cities had clubs in place prior to the explosion with established pools of comedians, so it was hard for new guys like me to get in. I started out doing a fifteen-minute routine to introduce the main act and had to work my way up from there. I had high ambitions for my career back then. I knew that when I was able to make $300 a week, I could say I had arrived!

So I traveled fifty weeks a year, trying to "make it." Within four or five years, I was headlining at clubs across the country—and partying pretty much every night. It was about this point in my life that I knew money wasn't going to make me happy. The three hundred dollars a week I was aiming for turned into five hundred a week, then $750 a week. At some point it got to two thousand a week, and I was still miserable. I figured out that it didn't matter how much I made—it would never be enough.

Down and Out in LA

Eventually, I moved to LA to chase my comedy dream. That's when my drinking really got out of hand. I chased the feeling of my first drink for years, and when alcohol couldn't do it, I chased it with drugs.

The first time I did cocaine, I had such a feeling of power and control. All my insecurities went away for a brief moment. I wanted that feeling again, but no matter how much I ingested, it never felt quite the same. It just left me feeling empty and desperate for more.

When I was in Pittsburgh one night, a dental student gave me my first taste of meth. I fell in love. But after that, I just couldn't find that drug anywhere. If meth had been as ubiquitous as it is today, I don't know where I would be now. But no matter how many times or how many different combinations of substances I tried to get back "there," I could never get that first-time feeling back. There was no "there" there.

Easy accessibility to drugs and alcohol was part of the comedy scene in the '80s. Some club owners even wanted to pay me in cocaine! I at least had sense enough to know that cocaine was not legal tender, no matter how much of it I used. I just knew in my heart that the phone company wouldn't take it for payment.

I fell into addiction without even looking where I was jumping. Once I was at a Denny's restaurant, chopping up cocaine on the table. The manager came over and said, "Are you crazy? That's a felony!" But I had no clue why he was so upset at that moment. I was just going with the flow. I gathered it all up and apologized, but I still didn't see what the big deal was. It was just what was done.

As it turned out, I didn't really like cocaine because I couldn't get what I wanted from it. I ended up using it so I could drink more and keep my mouth working. I was getting sloppy. As my tolerance level increased, which it always does with alcoholics, I had to find other ways to keep it effective, which usually meant finding speed or cocaine.

For example, when I was about to go on stage for the first time in Colorado Springs, I couldn't speak. People who live in those high-altitude areas will tell you that one drink in Denver is the same as two in Chicago. (The scientific proof is pretty scant, but it's hard to argue with experience.) I was blissfully unaware that altitude and alcohol are not a good mix. Both of them dehydrate you and decrease your reaction time—not good for someone who has to think on his feet and talk for an hour. I finished my first show sloppy and obviously drunk.

"Is this going to be a problem?" the club owner asked me.

"I don't get it," I told him. "All I had was my usual twelve beers." Rolling his eyes, he reminded me I was six thousand feet above sea level. At least the cocaine enabled me to talk.

I knew I wasn't headed in a good direction. I needed to grow up; if I kept on the path I was on, I was going to die sooner or later. So I started thinking that all my friends who were married had settled down and seemed to be happy—that must be it! I was going to get married.

I told my friends I needed a wife. In most circles, I'm the most cynical person I know; there was one bar I frequented where they even sarcastically called me "Mr. Sunshine." Those were the lucky people to hear my resolution one night from the bar stool where I was perched after a show: "I will be married in a year!"

"Who's going to marry you?!" they asked. In spite of their lack of confidence, I knew I could do this. I just needed to find a woman who didn't know me well.

I had given myself quite the challenging task. At the time, my dating life consisted of whoever I met at the club that week. We would hook up for a night, maybe two or three days, occasionally even four days, but that was it. Then I was off to the next city and the next unsuspecting female. For almost a decade, that was what I considered dating.

If there had been dating apps back then, my profile would have read: "Alcoholic drug addict with rage issues looking for a single woman willing to overlook aforementioned character flaws." The truth is, we hide those parts of ourselves from people until we can no longer keep them under wraps.

She Said "I Guess So"

After dating several of them, I swore off waitresses. God laughed and sent me to a comedy club in Ohio. As I was doing my show, I heard this beautiful laugh that seemed to move all over the room. I fell in love with that laugh. Tami was a smoker back then. I don't care what anyone says, smokers have the best laughs. When you can't get oxygen into your lungs, that is music to a comic's ear. I kept hearing these various gags and wheezes from the back of the room and thinking, *Holy cow, it's a woman, and she digs me. I am going to find out who this person is.*

After the show, I had to know who had such a unique laugh. "Who's the one that couldn't breathe? And is she still alive?" Everyone knew who I was asking about: the waitress who was changing her clothes after her shift. That's when I met Tami. *Holy cow! She's gorgeous! Short leather skirt, white blouse, five foot ten, and legs that seemed to go on forever.* It was the '80s, so she had gorgeous, permed hair. She coughed and a couple of doves flew out of it. It was a sign. This one was special.

So, I forgot about my "no waitresses" rule, even though I was only a week into my new commitment. Are you sensing a pattern in my life? No one lies to me more than me! I had also just quit drinking (again) a few days earlier. That didn't last much longer, either. I started right back up again and was impressed that Tami could actually keep up with my drinking pace. That was another rule I had: Any woman I went out with needed to fit into my lifestyle. She had to be able to drink and hold her liquor.

The reasons to be impressed just kept coming as I heard Tami's bio: a single mom of a two-year old boy, working two jobs, paying her own rent, and owned a car. I was struggling enough with just one job.

We hung out that entire week. As I flew back to Los Angeles, I thought, *This is different.* It wasn't like all the other one- to three-nighters I'd had. I actually wanted to see Tami again and get to know her better. We talked on the phone often, and I even visited Ohio. Occasionally, she would meet me in cities near Cleveland where I was performing.

That initial spark ignited in November 1985. The following January, I flew Tami and her son, Aaron, out to LA. We spent a week together doing all the LA things: We went to Disneyland; we went to the beach; we visited the La Brea tar pits; we checked out the Griffith Observatory; we hung around my incredibly dirty apartment; and she met some of my friends. It was like we were a married couple with a child. We did everything Aaron wanted to do. (He thought Mickey was his best friend, but Goofy was out to get him.) Playing dad for seven days convinced me I was ready to take the plunge into marriage and parenting. At the end of the week, Tami went back to Ohio.

As she told me many years later, I was the first comic she had ever dated, so she wasn't sure quite what to make of me for a while, but she felt I was someone she could trust. But she saw me more as a way out than the perfect catch. Her parents hadn't approved when she'd had a child outside of marriage, so she thought if she could find a decent guy who could legitimize her being a mother and give her a way not to have to work two jobs and be exhausted all the time, she'd be making progress. Somehow, she fooled herself into thinking I might actually make her life easier.

I saw her a few more times over the next several months. Then, on a red-eye flight to Ohio in April, I got the inspiration to ask her to marry me. So I did just that thirty minutes later at that Cleveland baggage claim.

Now, to be clear, I've paid the price for that proposal ever since. Every time we watch a movie where some guy does it right, gets down on one knee, says he asked the parents, pulls out a ring, and proposes in a beautifully special place, Tami starts crying. I always offer to ask her again and make it a better story this time, but she always says no and insists, "My story is the baggage claim. That's what I got."

But that's not all she got. As I said earlier, when she picked up the luggage that day, she had no idea the baggage that she was getting.

Not long after that memorable proposal, in one of those rare serious moments, my dad gave me one piece of advice on my wedding day: "Before you argue with your new wife—and you will argue with her—ask yourself this question." He paused dramatically. "Do you want to be right, or do you want to be happy?" Then he broke down sobbing in front of me.

Weird, I thought. *Thanks, Dad.*

I like to say that it took me a long time to choose to be happy. I haven't been right in years, but my wife assures me now that I'm very happy.

A month after I proposed, we found out Tami was pregnant. She came out of the bathroom crying. I, on the other hand, was ecstatic! *We're going to have a baby, how cool is that?!* Tami, having been there before, knew what that meant. Another baby was twice the responsibility she already had. I know after reading this far you can't possibly understand why she was concerned about yours truly. I remind you as I reminded her that day, I was ready to be a dad and a husband. At least I thought I was. Turns out I had no clue what all that entailed.

So, I proposed in April, she got pregnant in May, we married in July, and within a year I went from being single and traveling fifty weeks a year to married with two children under the age of four. *What could possibly go wrong?*

CHAPTER 4

Let the Spiral Begin

L et me just say, our honeymoon was amazing. I was scheduled for
a show in the Ozarks, so we decided to take advantage of my Four
Seasons hotel accommodations by having the trip double as our honeymoon. My beautiful bride was excited and couldn't wait to see our
hotel and enjoy some time by the lake.

As we pulled up to our destination, our jaws dropped. The Four
Seasons it was not. Not even close. Our luxurious lodging was a
converted double-wide trailer—a Deer Motel designed for hunters to
crash in for the night before heading out again the next morning. As
Tami discovered, marrying an up-and-coming comic didn't mean she
would always get a decent place to stay.

The amenities were nonexistent. But then, who really needs a
clean room? After all, it was convenient for Tami because she didn't
even need to get out of bed to reach the toilet when the morning
sickness hit her. And the pool? Let's just say it was tad small and
the murky water looked like it might double as a fishing hole.

Suffice to say that "relaxing" and "romantic" were two words that place did not bring to mind. More like "salmonella" and "staph infection."

We looked for activities, and I decided to play a round of golf. I shot an abysmal game, which was about the only thing above par the entire trip. As I unloaded my clubs from the cart afterward, we started chatting with a group of guys who then invited me out. So, of course, after dropping my new and pregnant wife off at the double-wide from Hell, I joined my new friends for a night of drinking. And joined them again the next night. And the next. Every night of our trip, I tossed back drinks during all hours of the night while Tami sat alone at our dingy motel, which I am sure did loads to abate her mounting anxiety about who she had just married.

I was already on my way to becoming Husband of the Year.

The Fall in Boston

Within the first month of our marriage, Tami and I moved to the hottest comedy scene in the country: Boston. The town was filled with clubs where a comedian could easily make a living. Even restaurants were converting their businesses into comedy places because that's where the money was. Just having a reputation that I was a regular in Boston could help take my career to the next level.

Since Tami and Aaron had been living in Ohio before we married, we had to transport their belongings northeast to our new home. With very little money to my name, I rented the smallest U-Haul trailer I could find. I told her we could take whatever fit in the trailer, but the rest would have to stay.

After cramming and rearranging Aaron's bedroom furniture into the tiny trailer as best I could, I realized nothing else was going to fit. No bed for us, no sofa or chairs, nothing.

I told Tami not to worry; I would buy new furniture when we got to Boston—one of many lies I would tell early on in our marriage. What she didn't know was that I had written a bad check to put down the security deposit on our new apartment.

"Don't you worry, babe. I'll get you a bed," I promised without knowing where I would get the money for it. I also neglected to mention that I had gotten only one show to prove myself to the powers that be in Boston. There would be no second chances.

I did well enough to book some time slots, but it took awhile to get into those, so I hit the road again.

Show after show, I got paid to make people laugh. But as soon as I got a check in my hand, I would pull up a seat at the bar and order my drink of choice, or covertly swap cash for cocaine. After a wild night of partying, I'd return to my comfortable hotel room and crash on the soft bed, only to do it all over again the next day.

Sometimes Tami would call to catch up, but it seemed like she was always nagging and irritating me.

"Jeff," my increasingly pregnant wife would say, "when you get home, could you get that bed you promised me? My back is really starting to bother me."

"Stop pestering me," I'd snap. "I said I would get you a bed, and I will—when I have the money."

I'd hang up feeling guilty and then rage out in my hotel room. *Why can't she just stay off my back about the bed! I don't have the money.* Then I'd step out to buy some cocaine.

After about a month of Tami sleeping on the floor, I did buy a bed. But I also kept shelling out a large portion of my earnings to support my habits. Cocaine became my ever-present friend. Every Friday, my dealer would come in with his Crown Royal bag full of quarters, halves, and grams. I'd line up with the other addicts like kids at a candy store, all eagerly waiting our turn to buy our drug of choice. And each week, I'd stand there and tell myself that I couldn't get drugs. I had a family, rent to pay, and mouths to feed. I needed to take the money and go. Yet each week, I'd hand my earnings over to the dealer for more cocaine. A little side note: the young man who sold us the coke every Friday and Saturday was later found strapped to a chair in his kitchen with a bullet in his head. I guess someone had paper out on him.

"It's Just Comedy!"

Everywhere I looked, I saw signs of my inadequacy as a man. I honestly had no idea what I expected to happen after I got married. I was flying by the seat of my pants, trying to hang on to my old life while "playing" at being a husband and father. If there was a written test on what good husbands and fathers were supposed to do, I would have failed miserably. I had no idea what personal sacrifice looked like. Looking back, those ideas about manhood were a recipe for disaster: Men were angry. Men drank. Men were not to be bothered with the daily minutiae of home life. All I had to do was bring home the money, pay the bills, and be left alone, right? Everything else was "her job." And Tami, of course, had her own ideas of what a husband and father should do.

But to be honest, I was failing at the one thing I told myself *was* my job: I wasn't making enough money to pay the bills. Well, I was, but I couldn't keep up with the bills and still buy booze and cocaine. I couldn't drink in the bars until 3:00 a.m. and still pay the rent. Something had to give.

Tami and the kids felt like constant reminders of how I was not only screwing up my life, but theirs as well. The combination of all those things planted new seeds in my already-crowded neurotic garden. The newest weed to grow was guilt—the one thing I had been able to live without up to that point. I rarely, if ever, felt guilty for any of my behavior. Not for landing myself in yet another drunk tank to sleep it off, the bar fights I got into, or even the DUIs I'd received. To me, those were all part of the drinker's life. Annoying, but nothing to feel guilty about. But that changed after I said, "I do." In hindsight, it was a good thing that I felt guilty: It meant that somewhere inside, I had a conscience. Unfortunately, my reaction to the guilt and shame I was feeling wasn't to change my behavior; I just raged out even more.

Every night, I lived the party life at the clubs, drinking too much and buying enough cocaine to keep me awake on stage and for the ride home. Those drives were when I'd start rethinking my life. I just wanted to run away from it all. Until that point, my relationships with women had ended when they got complicated. I think it was Scott Peck who wrote that true love cannot even begin in a relationship until conflict enters it. In other words, there is no such thing as a conflict-free relationship. The irony for me was that I hated conflict. My reaction to it was to flee: I fled from my father, my brother, and every woman I ever got involved with until Tami. But that option wasn't available now that I was married. I had made a commitment that was scaring the snot out of me. I was full of fear, loathing, and anger—a great cocktail of emotions to be in a relationship with.

I thought the road would be my sanctuary, the one place I could get away from my stress and guilt. But Tami constantly called to politely remind me that she needed money for groceries, the electric company called, the rent was past due—on and on. As I write this, it seems funny to me that as a thirty-year-old man, I just wanted to be left alone. A quick tip to the reader: If you want to be left alone, don't get married, and certainly don't have children.

So I would look at my responsibilities and feel guilty, which would trigger shame, which would trigger rage. Wash, rinse, repeat. Not exactly a recipe for a peaceful, loving home. I needed to come up with a plan. Alcoholics Anonymous has a saying: "You are the reason you are here." In other words, maybe the psychotic drunks aren't the best at figuring out the solutions to their own problems, since their choices created many of their problems in the first place.

But being the genius I was, I came up with a plan to fix everything. I decided I needed to get Tami to leave me. I wasn't man enough to just say it wasn't working and that we should cut our losses. I wanted her to leave me so that years later I could point the finger at her and say, "*You* were the one who left *me*."

So I lashed out to drive her away—but she wasn't going anywhere. I married a tough woman who wasn't putting up with *anything*. When I would come home drunk at three in the morning, I'd crawl into bed, hoping to sleep until I could get back to the party. But she'd wake up each morning, plant her feet on my rear end, and shove me out of bed onto the floor, telling me to get up because our children needed a father. And I hated her for it.

It's been said that an alcoholic will remain emotionally at the stage of development they were at when they start drinking. I don't know if that's true, but my behavior and attitude certainly reminded me of a thirteen-year-old. I tried to hang on to my old life. I didn't understand being married is all about give and take. All I was doing was taking, so everyone around me had to suffer as my downward spiral continued.

Despite my personal troubles, I still needed to get up on stage and make other people laugh. Tami would often call half an hour before the show, and we'd get into a huge argument. I'd hit the stage with rage boiling inside me and pour it out into my comedy. My comic friends would even ask me why I took her calls before the show because they always made me such a raging wreck. But because I had decided my marriage was causing all my problems, I made it the focus of my comedy. And it worked. I just poured out all the anger and bile on stage to get a laugh.

One of the most popular stories I told was about a roasted chicken. It was inspired by real events, although I took a lot of creative license. As I told it then, Tami had put a chicken in the roaster for dinner and asked me to carve it when it was ready. "Yeah, yeah, sure . . . whatever," I said. But I was tired and went to take a nap. When she tried to wake me up to carve the chicken, I just waved her off and rolled over. "I'm sleeping. Don't bother me."

"You said if I cooked the chicken, you'd carve it for me," she said, "so get up and carve the chicken!" Suffice to say, it didn't go well from there.

After I stumbled angrily from bed into the kitchen, we shouted at each other a lot, and the chicken ended up on the floor before I finally yelled, "You want me to carve your chicken? I'll carve it right here!" Then I stomped the chicken into the garbage disposal and ground it up while screaming at her, "You want your ****ing chicken? Here's your ****ing chicken!"

Occasionally, Tami would come to my shows. After hearing me rant about how awful she was, she'd run out to the parking lot, upset by my jabbing remarks. One night on the drive home, she told me, "You must really hate me."

"It's just comedy," I replied. But it wasn't. I was miserable, and I used my show as an outlet for that misery. Several female comedy club owners refused to invite me back during those years because I was so brutal toward my wife and women in general.

A Series of Unfortunate Events

Boston was supposed to be where my big breakthrough in comedy took place and life finally came together for us. We were supposed to finally "arrive" there—whatever that meant. But it didn't exactly work that way, thanks to my self-destructive behavior.

One night as I pushed through the front doors of a club into the street, laughter from my latest quip spilled out with me. I strode to my car to head home. I opened the door, slid into the driver's seat, leaned my head back against the headrest, and pulled my cocaine from my pocket. I started to lay out a couple of bumps for the ride home. Then . . .

Tap. Tap. Tap.

I instinctively shoved the coke onto the floor of the car and turned to see who was bothering me. I rolled down my window, blinded by a light. As I blinked several times, the light shifted enough to reveal a man wearing a crisp, dark police uniform.

CRAP! Did he see the drugs??

"Please get out of the car, sir," he commanded authoritatively. I started shaking right away. As I slowly stepped out onto the street, I felt his hands turn me against the car and cool metal handcuffs slap against my wrists. *Clickety-click.* And just like that, I had gone from cracking jokes to wearing cuffs.

As he turned me to face him, I just looked at the officer, but no words came out. I could vaguely hear him speaking, but what he was saying didn't register at first. Then he shined the light into the car and radioed his partner, "Yes, he was doing cocaine."

"Sir," he said to me. "Do you have any more drugs on you?"

I managed to shake my head and mumble, "No."

I shuffled alongside him as he led me to his cruiser and opened the back door. As I sat on the cold, vinyl seat with my cuffed hands crammed into the cushion behind me, thoughts swirled in my head: *I have a six-month-old and a three-year-old. I haven't even celebrated my first wedding anniversary yet. How many years will it be until I see them again?*

From the corner of my eye, I saw the shadowy figure of a man exit the club with a cigarette in his hands. I didn't realize it at the time, but it was an off-duty policeman who worked security at the club. As he lit up, he asked the arresting officer why I was in the car. Upon hearing that I was doing coke, he motioned the officer closer.

"Look, he's one of the comedians at the club, let him go," he said, as if that was a get-out-of-jail-free card. (Turns out, it was. *Holy cow!*)

After chatting with the off-duty cop a few more minutes, the officer turned back toward me and opened the door. "Come on, pal," he said as he turned me around and removed the cuffs. He told me how lucky I was: the district attorney was up for re-election and loved parading suburban white boys in front of the camera during the campaign.

"You were looking at three to five for possession," he said casually. "Have a nice night."

For most people, that close call would have sobered them up and driven them directly to the straight and narrow. But I was way too smart for that. I was only near my bottom, not quite "there" yet.

Just two nights later, I staggered out of a club in the wee hours, extremely drunk. But I decided I was still fully capable of driving. So I slid behind the wheel and headed for home.

After driving for a while, something just seemed off. The route didn't look the same as it usually did, but I couldn't quite figure out what was different as I pulled onto the interstate. There were only a few cars, but they all seemed to be driven by crazy folks. They kept shining their lights right in my eyes, even flashing them at me. I cussed them out a few times and swerved to miss them until it hit me: I was driving the wrong way on the interstate, right into oncoming traffic!

My only saving grace was that it was three o'clock in the morning, so there wasn't much other traffic. So I pulled off the interstate and found a different way home. But even then, I got turned around and went nearly all the way to Cape Cod before realizing I had made another mistake. I only lived forty minutes from the club, but it took me two hours to get home that night. Yet, somehow, I still made it home alive.

Bouncing off the Bottom

Despite these close calls, it never occurred to me to consider changing anything about my lifestyle. Tami and I went to a friend's July 4th party and enjoyed a great time in the sun, picnicking and celebrating. As evening fell, Tami told me she needed to get the kids home and that I needed to go with her.

"No, you take the kids home. I'll get a ride later," I told her. She sighed and trudged off, collected the kids, and headed home alone.

Finally, around 2:30 the next morning, I got a ride home. I stood alone in my dark living room, not wanting to go into the bedroom because I felt an enormous weight of guilt and shame. Once again, the fight-or-flight instinct was coursing through my veins. I wanted out. I couldn't breathe. Years later, I told a friend who had the same demons I had that he would come home one night, look at his wife and children, and do one of two things: he would either sober up and take care of his responsibilities, or flee. I found out a few months later that he fled to San Francisco. Only the ocean stopped him from getting further away.

This night was my moment to decide. I stood there, perplexed, trying to figure out where it was coming from because I'd never felt like that before. So I did what I always did: I got out some rum and started drinking, then added some cocaine to "help me think straight."

I started writing in a journal to process my thoughts . . . and then it hit me:

It all started when I got married. I'm not even a year into this marriage, and look what has happened to me. It's all her fault. I'm done. I've got to get out of this thing. What should I do?

Then I had another brilliant thought: *If I beat her up, she'll have to divorce me. No woman could stay with a guy who would do that to her.* There is a reason the first step in a twelve-step program is acknowledging your insanity. This was insane, but the more I dwelled on it, the more it made sense.

I knocked down a couple more shots and inhaled a couple more lines of coke as I processed that. Finally, I was ready to do it. I would drag Tami out of bed and beat her so she would have to leave me, and I would be alone. *And happy again? Who knows?*

I walked down the short hallway and into the bedroom. I stood over my sleeping wife, my hands clenched as I felt the anger building inside me. A little voice told me this was wrong, very wrong. But I'd already made up my mind. I knew what I had to do.

I reached down to pull her from the bed—and just then our seven-month-old son, Ryan, started crying. I instinctively moved to the crib to try to quiet him down, but he wouldn't stop the noise. He just got louder and louder. *Make it stop!*

All that rage and frustration welled up within me as I pulled my hand back and then slapped his diaper. Repeatedly.

Whack. Whack. Whack.

Tami jumped out of bed, pushed past me, and grabbed the baby. I started to follow her down the hall, about to apologize, when she turned on the hall lights and I saw Ryan staring back at me over her shoulder. His eyes were full of fear. And I had put that fear there. The realization of what I had done, what I might have done—it all hit me so hard I couldn't breathe. To this day, I believe that boy took a beating for his mother.

Eventually, Tami walked back into the bedroom and sat on the end of the bed. As she began feeding the baby, he quieted down. He was hungry, cried to get fed, and got beaten because he was hungry. What kind of man does that?

"Tami," I said, choking back tears, "if you don't take me to Alcoholics Anonymous, I won't go. But if I don't go, we're not going to make it." I turned toward her as the tears began to flow. "I need help."

She didn't disagree. Years later, I shared this story publicly for the first time. Ryan was twelve years old, and he came up to me after hearing it. He asked, "Daddy, was I that boy?" I told him he was, and that I'm a different man today. He put his arms around me and said, "I forgive you."

Wow. Think of how different our lives would be if more fathers and sons could say that.

CHAPTER 5

"Daddy, You Win."

I n my very first Alcoholics Anonymous meeting, a guy walked over
to me with *The Big Book of Alcoholics Anonymous* and pointed to
the third-step prayer. "This is the prayer you pray every day," he said.
It read:

> God, I offer myself to Thee—to build with me and to do
> with me as Thou wilt. Relieve me of the bondage of self,
> that I may better do Thy will. Take away my difficulties,
> that victory over them may bear witness to those I would
> help of Thy Power, Thy Love, and Thy Way of Life.

"Congratulations," he said with a smile, "You won a raffle. The
book is yours to keep!" (I was pretty sure that was what they told all
the new people.) But as he turned away, he added, "Embrace the
Serenity Prayer, as well. It wasn't written just for alcoholics. It's for

people who need to change their ways and accept the things that cannot be changed."

That comment intrigued me, so I flipped through my new copy of *The Big Book* until I found the Serenity Prayer: "God, grant me the serenity to accept the things I cannot change, the courage to change the things I can, and the wisdom to know the difference." I recited the prayer softly to myself for the first time. I had no idea what I was saying, but with the image of Ryan's fearful eyes burned into my mind, I had decided to do whatever these people told me.

Every day, I prayed those two prayers. Some days I prayed to God—Who or Whatever that was. Some days, I prayed to the universe. Some days, I just screamed it into the void. But I prayed those prayers every day. July 5th became my own Independence Day. For the first time in a long time, I was sober.

But staying that way wasn't easy. The fact that I had quit drinking didn't make my demons disappear. One month into sobriety, I found myself sitting at a bar in Florida with a bottle of beer in front of me, daring myself not to drink it. On the one hand, I thought drinking it would offer me relief from white-knuckling my way through life the way I had been for the last month. On the other hand, if I did drink it, I could lose everything. As I sat there wrestling with whether or not to take that sip of beer, a man walked up behind me and tapped me on the shoulder.

"Hey, man. I saw your show," he said, sliding onto the stool next to me. "Is all that stuff about being an alcoholic true?"

"It is," I said, shaking my head and grimacing a little at the admission.

"Then what's that?" he asked, pointing to the beer bottle in front of me.

"Suicide," I replied.

"Let's go, man," he said, placing his hand on my shoulder as he stood. I eyed him questioningly. "We're going to a midnight meeting."

That guy was an angel sent to intervene that night; I am sure of it. I don't mean he had wings under his shirt or anything like that—just that he was in the right place at the right time and took action. And that it was no accident. This was the beginning of what would later form my faith.

AA leaders told us repeatedly there are no coincidences. I had no understanding of that, but time and again, people would show up at the right time to keep me on the path. I began to pay attention to the people who entered and exited my life. A saying here, a reprimand there, and more often than not, it helped me. I didn't always heed the advice I was given, but over time I began to realize that the people in those meetings knew a lot more about my alcoholism than I did.

Maybe there *was* something to praying.

After that midnight AA meeting in Tampa, I returned to saying my prayers every day with a renewed commitment to sobriety. They say to take sobriety one day at a time. Sometimes it can be one minute at a time, but you don't know what that really means until you're sitting there, staring at a cold beer.

Sick and Tired

A month and a half later, I was performing at a club in Memphis when an old coke buddy of mine showed up. "Good to see ya, man," he said as he dropped a bag of it on the table. When I saw the coke, every ounce of strength I'd regained in Tampa and every sober day since then just dissipated.

Just like that, I was in a bathroom stall, desperately snorting the coke. I threw my head back as it hit. I felt alive again! The energy of that feeling drowned out any regret in the moment. I had not one thought of my family or the troubles I would bring them. Back and back I went, until the bag was almost empty.

At one point my buddy and I were standing in front of Elvis's house, Graceland, screaming for the King. When the guard came out to tell us we had to wait until morning to see "the king," I said, "I was just wondering if Elvis, before he passed, might have perhaps left some Valium under the bushes, 'cause I am jacked!" So security threatened to call the police if we didn't leave.

I ended up back in my hotel room around 2:30 a.m., starting to come down from my high. I was sitting on the edge of a musty couch with an almost-empty coke bag on the table in front of me. As shame and despair began surfacing, I held my head in my hands and started to sob. I could only think that I was about to lose *everything*. Those feelings of guilt and shame were roaring back, as was the fear that I would never get free from this prison.

Oh well, I thought as I rubbed my forehead and ran my fingers through my hair, *screw it. Might as well finish it now.*

What I have learned about this kind of relapse is that once you start down the wrong path, you tend to feel like you might as well go all in. The little devil on your shoulder tells you just to go for it. It's as though once your toe is hanging off the sobriety ledge, you feel as if you might as well jump all in.

So I poured what remained of my friend's coke onto the table. I pulled my driver's license out of my wallet to chop it into lines—and as I did so, the phone number of an AA member back in Boston fell onto the table. I picked it up along with my license and sat staring at both for the next thirty minutes. I had to choose.

At 3:00 a.m., I picked up the phone and dialed the number on the business card. The guy answered groggily, and I told him the whole story.

"Are you serious about quitting?" he asked me.

"I am," I replied honestly, my forehead buried in the palm of my hand. "I'm soooo sick of this!"

"Do you have any coke left?" he asked.

I said I had a little less than a gram left. He said if I was serious about quitting, I would flush the coke down the toilet.

After a brief pause, he asked, "Did you flush the coke?"

"I did."

"Really? You're the first!" He was laughing. "You don't sound suicidal."

I told him I wasn't. I was just sick and tired of living that way.

"Great," he said. "New rules. From now on, call me *before* you use."

"Maybe You're the Problem."

Thus September 29, 1987, became my new official sobriety date, and Dick D. became my first sponsor. If he told me to do something, I did it.

I was still doing over two hundred shows a year, most of which were in nightclubs surrounded by drinkers. I remember someone once slipped vodka into my orange juice, thinking he was doing me a favor. I spit it across the bar and screamed at the man.

Later on, I went to a meeting and told the story. Someone asked what I had been doing in a bar when I was trying to stay sober. I said I was there to work; the guy suggested I quit my job. I told him I wasn't attending meetings to get career advice, I was just trying to figure out how to live my life without using alcohol, and if they couldn't help me, I didn't need to be going to those meetings.

I was making it one day at a time, but barely. I was whining about not being able to drink anymore while observing all the other people around me who were, when my sponsor gave me the best piece of information I have ever gotten: "Who says you can't drink?" he asked.

"You're a big boy. Nobody is going to stop you. Just think it through and know what the total cost of that drink is." He was right on—it wasn't the few dollars that the drink cost, it was losing Tami and the kids, my home, and possibly my life. Those were not costs I was willing to pay. It gave me something other than my self-pity to cling to in those hard times when I wanted to drink.

Even though I was doing the work, my life didn't really look that much better. Frustration still defined me, and rage still consumed me. And I still thought my marriage was what was causing my unhappiness.

About eighteen months into my new sobriety period, a little old lady made her way over to me after one of my local meetings. "Young man," she said as she poked me in the navel, "I've been listening to you complain about your wife at every meeting. 'That woman this,' and 'that woman that.'" She looked up and straight into my eyes. "Maybe the problem in your life isn't your wife. Maybe it's you."

I wanted to pound her noggin into her chest cavity. I didn't like hearing that at all, but I couldn't exactly avoid jail time if I raged out on a little old lady, so I took it like a man. Which to me, at that time, meant to bottle it up and ignore it. But it registered that I had been complaining about my home life for more than a year before someone had the nerve to suggest that maybe I was the problem in my marriage. I had never really considered that option before.

Every time Tami and I argued, my fight-or-flight reflex kicked in. I had no desire for conflict, but I couldn't stop myself from yelling the loudest anytime we argued. Like my father, I broke things. I smashed things.

Looking back now, I am amazed that Tami stayed with me. As I've come to understand, even in recent years, she was wrestling with her own demons, too. I realize now that we were both responding to childhood trauma in many different and unhealthy ways. Deep down, we both had such low self-esteem that we didn't think we deserved any better than each other.

It's been said that hurt people hurt people. We were both reacting to hidden wounds, but I confess I was the one handing out the most pain in those years.

Tirade on a Stool

After about two years in Boston, we moved to New Jersey so I could work at the New York comedy clubs. New York was my next big place to "make it." If I could tenure in a club in NYC, television executives could discover me. I could find my big break. So, several nights a week, I'd commute into the city to perform.

I don't know if New York City is exactly where one goes to get sober. I was told you need three AA meetings a day just to deal with the idiots you meet at the bus stop. I will say it was a different culture of sobriety: honest and raw. It was the first place I heard the phrase "you lie, you die." In other words, you are only as sick as your secrets. But transparency will keep you healthy. So you would hear things like, "I stabbed my wife this morning, but I didn't drink." Then six other guys would say, "Oh I remember when I did that. . . ." What?

I may not have been using alcohol, but my frustration and anger continued to rear their ugly heads. People often think if they get sober, life will improve, but that's not how it happened for me. I'm the reason AA is anonymous: They didn't want me as their poster boy because I was still such a jerk.

But I will say AA was the first place I saw the face of God. Those people accepted me as I was—foul-mouthed, angry, and bitter. They always greeted me with a hug and a smile and would say, "Hang in there. Don't give up before the miracle." I would say, "Shut up" as I laughed.

I was working the program, and it was changing me.

Owning what came out of my mouth was a huge game changer for me. I was raised by a man who never apologized for anything he said. So imagine my surprise when I was told I had go back and apologize to people I had said things to. That would be the ninth of the twelve steps I was trying to live by: "Make direct amends to such people wherever possible, except when to do so would injure them or others."

One particular incident took place at my local bank. I lashed out at the teller because she "had the nerve" to bounce several of my checks. I reacted to that "outrage" by saying several nasty things to the unsuspecting lady. Security all but threw me out of the bank.

When I told my sponsor about it, he said I had to go back and apologize. I said, "Why? I can just change banks." He said if I ran from the responsibility of asking for forgiveness, I would never get well. So I went back to the bank and very sheepishly walked up to the teller who not two hours earlier I had belittled. I told her I had been out of line and asked if she would forgive me. She initially tensed up, getting ready to attack when she saw me walk in, but after the apology she very politely said, "Thank you."

It didn't cure me right away, but like everything in recovery, it was a baby step toward becoming whole.

The "cheese incident" is another example of what life was like with me. I wanted a snack, so I opened the fridge to browse my options and saw two packages of cheese—one opened pack with a little left, and a brand-new one.

I have a phobia about used dairy. If I have no idea how long it has been sitting around, I won't eat it. Since I didn't know how long that particular hunk of cheese had been in our fridge, I tossed it out and opened the new one.

Then Tami walked in and said, "There was an already opened package. Use that one first before opening the new one."

"I saw that open one, but I don't want it," I told her. "Who knows how long it's been in there?"

"It was perfectly fine," she replied.

"Then you can have it. I will eat this one."

"I don't want it."

"Neither do I!" I yelled.

It escalated to the point where I was standing on a stool screaming at the top of my lungs, "I DON'T WANT IT! Are you ****ing deaf?!"

Tami dropped to her knees and started weeping.

Later that evening, I went to tuck Aaron into bed. "Daddy, you win," he whispered as I tucked the blanket around him.

"What do you mean, bud? Win what?"

"You yell. Mommy cries. You win."

That was not one of my prouder moments as a man. I headed back downstairs, found Tami still wiping away the tears, and told her I needed help.

"You think?" she said. From the look on her face, I was pretty sure she didn't believe I was being serious.

That night, I went to a late AA meeting and asked the group if they knew of a decent therapist. Someone recommended one named Joanne, and I called her the next morning.

Trouble's Coming

If you are looking to get well, I suggest finding a therapist who works for the state. At fifteen dollars an hour, those people are not in it for the money. And at that rate, they don't suffer liars and fools; they want to see results. But my naïve self really thought I could fool Joanne.

On my first day of therapy, I knew what I wanted: Permission to get a divorce. I wanted Joanne to hear my tale of woe, pat me on the hand, and say, "You poor man! You need to get away from that woman."

So I told her my tale, and she said, "If you came here looking for permission to divorce your wife, you came to the wrong therapist." It's as if she looked straight into my heart and knew me inside and out. I stammered out something to the effect of "No, I just want to get well. I have issues."

My first question was, "When will I be done with this?" I wanted to know when I would get "there."

Joanne told me it was pretty simple: At that moment, I was making some pretty crappy choices based on faulty information. The plan was to change the information I was working with so I could make better choices. In other words, I would become my own therapist.

Sounds simple, right? It's not.

Tami and I tried to attend counseling together, but we couldn't sit in the same room for more than five minutes without bickering to the point of no return. In our first session, Joanne asked me if I loved Tami. I replied, "I guess, in the way I love my sister." Tami told me years later that was the most hurtful thing I ever said to her. Joanne must have agreed because she separated us, sending me to the hallway.

After a little while, Tami walked out, sobbing. One of the things Joanne asked was what our goals for counseling were. Tami's response was: "I want Jeff to be the way he was when we were dating. He was so much nicer then."

"That's not realistic," Joanne answered. "It'll never be the way it was when you were dating." And Tami cried. The truth is that for married people, things can never be like they were when you were dating; that is an illusion God created to keep the species going.

Eventually, Tami stopped going to counseling because, as she said, "All I do is cry."

A few months into our sessions, Joanne asked me again, "Do you love your wife?"

I sat there for a few moments, flummoxed. I decided to embrace the whole "being honest" thing.

"I'm not sure."

"Listen, Jeff," she said, leaning forward to emphasize her point, "I think you love her very much. I don't think you'd be here, going through what you're going through to become a better man and to claim a better marriage, if you didn't."

I took it in, but was a bit taken aback. *What if she was right?* Then as I drove home, I started to think how broken I must be to need someone to *tell* me I was in love. Shouldn't a person know that? That's how "frozen" I was. It was as if I was in a cryogenic state, but still awake.

The little old lady's words from the club came back to haunt me. *What if I am the problem?* For the first time, I began looking at my marriage differently. Instead of viewing Tami as the only problem, I felt that I was damaged, too. And my feeling of hopelessness grew.

I started to read voraciously—mostly books Joanne recommended. Like a lot of men, I felt if I was as broken as I knew myself to be, then there must be a manual to help fix it somehow. I started with *The Road Less Traveled* by M. Scott Peck. For the first time, I thought, *That's good stuff. Maybe there are answers to my questions somewhere.* The first line in the book states that life is difficult. Peck argues that when we can accept that fact, life no longer feels as difficult. It just becomes a series of problems that need to be solved. *Wow,* I thought. *That makes sense, I just need to figure out how to solve the problems of my life.* The problem was, most of my problems were self-inflicted.

That book started me on a journey of reading and searching for answers that lasted several years. I would read a book and get all excited, thinking perhaps I had found them. Then as I tried living out what I learned, that feeling would dissipate. So I'd get another book and start all over again. It was like my soul was extremely thirsty—even parched—but every time I thought I'd found some water, I didn't have a cup to hold it. So all I could do was scoop a little up with my hands. Most of the water I thought I had found trickled through my fingers before I could even get it to my lips—and what I did manage to swallow didn't really quench my thirst. In many ways, it just made me even thirstier, knowing that other people seemed to be finding answers, but none of them really worked for me. So I kept reading, hoping to find someone, somewhere, who got it and could point me to water I could drink that would help me never be thirsty again.

One day, Tami and I got into a particularly heated argument in our bedroom. We were both yelling, as usual, trying to outdo each other. She picked up something and threw it at me. Something hard and metallic hit me square in the face. And my rage just exploded.

I flew across the room and grabbed her by the throat. But Tami had been in an abusive relationship before meeting me, and she wasn't going to take any of that. She started hitting me with all her might.

I just dropped my arms and let her hit me, stunned by my own actions. I knew I deserved it.

Eventually, things calmed down, so I just sat on the end of the bed. Ryan, then four, came to me with a little book and tried to get me to read it to him. "Look, Dad. It's very funny. Ha ha!" When I blew him off, he left me alone. But soon, Tami and I were fighting once again in the bedroom when we heard a lamp crash in the living room.

"What was that?" She turned toward the noise. But I already knew what it was because of what I had learned in my therapy sessions and the books I'd been reading.

"That's our son trying to break up our fight."

"What are you talking about?"

"Our yelling is too much for him, so he broke a lamp."

"Why would he do that?"

"So we'd have to stop fighting to go see what happened," I explained. "Today it's the lamp, tomorrow it's drugs or alcohol or liquor store robberies." I turned toward Tami and said, "If we don't get this in check, our kids are going to be in trouble."

"That's nonsense," she said.

I must confess, I had never given her any reason to put any confidence in anything I said. But this time I actually knew what I was talking about. I had read about how kids take on different roles within the family dynamic to cope.

I went downstairs and, sure enough, there was the broken lamp and Ryan.

"What happened?" I asked.

"I don't know, Dad," he replied. "It was an accident."

"An accident." I nodded and put my arm around him. "Okay, it was an accident. I know it's hard to hear your mom and dad fight, isn't it?"

He just nodded and leaned into my hug.

Dazed and Confused

Despite my best efforts, without alcohol and cocaine, the anger just kept pouring out of me. I was snotty, sarcastic, and bitter. I knew it wasn't healthy. I knew it wasn't right. I knew it wasn't good. I just didn't know why I was like that.

I'd wake up every day, look around, take inventory of my life, and find everything was "there"—a beautiful wife, loving children, even a job I loved at one point—but I was still full of anxiety and didn't know why.

I felt alone. I knew Tami did, too. Why wouldn't she? We argued over *everything*. The New York City clubs weren't happening for me. Everyone was wondering what had happened to me. The word on the street was that I'd quit drinking and wasn't funny anymore.

So Tami and I did what we did when the going got tough: We moved.

CHAPTER 6

A Dry, Deserted Place

After two years in New Jersey, Tami started wanting us to buy a house of our own—something she could make into a home that was better than the various rentals we had been inhabiting. I agreed. But the problem was we were in New Jersey, which isn't exactly cheap. I knew I was going to have a problem when I saw a full-page ad in the Sunday paper that said, "Affordable starter homes, starting at $495,000!" Affordable for *whom*? I jokingly told Tami I might be able to afford a room above the garage of one of those places.

My sister, who was living in Arizona, called me one day and said the state was literally giving houses away due to a housing market collapse. So I told Tami that we could move to Arizona. We convinced ourselves that we were struggling in our lives because Los Angeles, not New York, was actually the place we needed to be for sitcoms and comedy opportunities to find us. We naïvely thought it would be easier and less expensive for me to fly from Phoenix to LA for thirty dollars. Like everything in my life up to that point, there was no plan. Just an idea and an impulse to get moving. I thought when life gets too uncomfortable where you are, the solution is to pack up and move, whether it makes sense or not. The important thing is to tell the right lies to yourself and rationalize it. As happens so often in life, things look better on paper than in practice.

I figured since Tami was going to spend a heck of a lot more time in the house than I would, she should make the decision about which one to buy. I flew her out alone on a Thursday to look at houses, and by Saturday, she said we had one. I never laid eyes on it until the moving truck arrived. Thankfully, the house met our needs, and we settled right into the arid atmosphere of Arizona. Somehow the environment seemed to fit my stage of life.

We moved in in November, and the weather in Phoenix that time of year is beautiful. But by the following August, Tami was dying from the heat. I came home from the golf course one day during the monsoon season to find my beautiful wife standing in the driveway, soaking wet, arms outstretched, just absorbing all that rain. As I was getting out of the car, she said, "Look, Jeff, it actually rains in this godforsaken place!" That was the first of many clues she dropped that made me believe we weren't done moving.

I continued traveling for my comedy shows and stayed on the road longer than I stayed at home, so at least Tami and the kids got a lot of breaks from me. During my trips, I'd often sit in the quiet of my hotel room during the day and ponder the many questions that plagued my soul: *Where did we go wrong? What am I missing?* I tried journaling and mapping my life out on paper, but none of it seemed to help.

At one point, I tried a practice I had heard about: writing my own obituary and what I'd want my family to say about me at my funeral. But I never got past the first line: "He always had time for us." That broke me. I needed to find some answers—and quickly.

I once got wrapped up for a couple of days just staring at the kids' gerbil. At some point, Tami asked me what was up with me and the gerbil.

"Look at that thing."

She said, "So what?"

"Watch it. It gathers up sticks on one side of the cage and brings them over to the other side. Then when that's done, he repeats the process and brings them back to the other side. Every now and then, he spins that wheel for entertainment."

She repeated herself. "So *what*?"

"That's our life!" I told her. "I go to work and make some money. We buy some things, and they wear out. We take them to the landfill. If I am lucky, I land a sitcom or movie deal, and we get to buy nicer things, but eventually they all wear out and we take them to the landfill. Every now and then we take the kids to Disneyland or go to Vegas—that's our wheel of entertainment. But in the end, it always leaves us empty."

"What are you talking about?" she said, perplexed.

"I am looking ahead, babe, projecting my life for the next fifteen or twenty years. If all it is is gathering *sticks*, I'm checking out!"

She replied, "You checked out years ago, pal!"

I then asked her, "Don't you ever wonder?"

"Wonder what?"

"Why are we here? What's the point to all this?"

She said, "Not really, Jeff. I don't have time. I am raising a family virtually alone. You signed on to do things, and you're not doing them! We are losing *everything*!"

It was a sad conversation. But I still couldn't figure out why gathering any of the sticks of life should matter.

"We are losing the house, and I get the impression you don't even care!" she continued.

"I don't."

"Who says that?!" she exclaimed.

"A person who doesn't care," I replied impassively. "I *want* to care. Do you honestly think I wake up in the morning, look at all of this responsibility—the mortgage, the food, the clothing, the car—and don't think that the fact it is all sliding away from me means I should probably care about it? But I don't know why it all matters."

At one point I bought a car that Ford had no business selling me. There was no way I could make the payments. So a few months later, I stopped making them because it was either pay for the house or the car. One day, Tami called me when I was on the road and said, "They just came and repossessed the car. You knew this was coming and you said nothing, you coward!" Try explaining to your children why a strange man is taking their daddy's car.

I don't know if anyone reading this knows what it's like to wake up every day and realize how pointless everything in your life is. It creates a crippling anxiety. But everyone else around me seemed happy. What was *wrong* with me?

Not only was Tami doing everything at the house, she was also doing side jobs like cleaning other people's houses in what little extra time she had to improve our bottom line. I knew something had to change; I just didn't know what.

At one point, I was reading about Eastern mysticism and came home with another "revelation" for Tami.

"I want to raise the kids to be Buddhist," I said. The kids were around seven and nine years old at the time. "I'm going to put the kids in a school run by a Buddhist monastery." I was certain this was the answer.

"Have you lost your mind?" she asked.

"No, no, no," I insisted, "it makes sense." The way I had it figured, every man in my family had been a rage freak with out-of-control anger that hurt everyone. "These Buddhist monks seem pretty calm. When was the last time you read about a Buddhist monk road-rage incident?"

I wasn't even sure Buddhist monks drove cars. But it made as much sense as anything else. I was definitely grasping at straws.

Tami just shook her head and declared, "You're not putting my kids in a Buddhist monastery."

"All right," I said. And that was the end of that. It took her less than three minutes to talk me out of that one.

Bouncing off the Bottom Again

Instead of getting better as I navel-gazed, our marriage continued to disintegrate over the next several years. My career seemed to have plateaued. I had hoped to make it big by that point but felt stuck, unable to break through to higher-caliber venues. Part of the problem was that my agent at the time had convinced me that all I was ever going to be was a second-class comedian, so I needed to be happy with what I could get. It wasn't exactly the kind of supportive behavior I should have expected from an agent, but it fit the negative script playing on repeat in my own head, so I accepted it as probably true. And acted accordingly.

Another problem was that the demand for comedians was declining overall. When we moved to Arizona, clubs were paying comedians at my level $1,500 to $2,500 for a week of performances. It used to be that they would pay airfare, accommodations, and expenses on the trips, but they started tightening the fiscal belt as the market got more demanding.

First, the airfares went away. That meant I had to use part of whatever I earned to buy my own ticket to the venue. That hurt a lot. Some of them were connected to hotels or apartments where I could stay for free, but those that weren't soon stopped paying for hotel costs, too. That effectively cut my income in half.

Then they started cutting the core stipend I got for a week's work, which dramatically cut into my bottom line. I watched the money I got slide from $2,500 to $1,500. *Whoa,* I thought, *how am I going to make ends meet now?* Then it slipped to $1,250. *Sheesh!* And finally, the stipend slid all the way down to only $1,000 for a week of comedy. After paying my own airfare and all other expenses, I was pretty much working for free. The numbers just didn't add up. The owner of the Comedy Cottage had been right: I was a zero-dollar comic!

I even stopped paying taxes because I just didn't have any money left over to give to the government. All the financial pressure just amped up the stress.

I started carrying this stuff onto the stage. It all came to head at a club in Portland. I was doing my show, and for whatever reason I started talking about how the government was hounding me for money, and I went off on everything. It was not even remotely funny—just an angry man spewing about all his problems. When the club owner got on a mic offstage and told me to leave, people cheered. It was the only time in my entire career that happened.

But I didn't leave the stage. I just kept ranting. Finally, an old lady in the front row said, "Why don't you shut up?"

My eloquent response was, "Lady, looking at you, your tax-paying days are over." That was it. Everyone in the room got up and started walking out. I took the hint and decided to finally leave, too.

I walked out into the lobby, and the old lady walked over to me, pointed at the top of my head, and said, "Young man, you are rotten from the tip of your head to the bottom of your feet." I walked into the office, and the owner told me how much money this was going to cost me in refunds. It was a humiliating experience. I started really thinking that I had to get out of comedy before I hurt someone and could possibly go to jail.

So I started to explore other ways to make money outside of comedy. Meanwhile, Tami helped us get by with her side gig cleaning houses and took a job as a receptionist at a radio station in Phoenix.

I thought maybe sales was something I might be able to do. Years before comedy, I took a job selling cars. It didn't go that well, but I was young. After a month of not selling a car, the sales manager came in and reminded me that I hadn't sold a car, to which I replied, "I don't think they want one."

He told me to go home and sit by the phone and he would call me when they got a customer who wanted a car. (That was over forty years ago—and he hasn't called me yet.)

But I was older now, and thought I had a little more incentive to sell vehicles. So I answered an ad in the newspaper for a dealership looking for a salesman.

I had three interviews for a job selling trucks. The managers asked me all kinds of questions and explored the reasons behind my answers. One guy asked me if there was anything in my life I was ashamed of. *Where does one begin?* I didn't think the guy had an hour, so I picked one of the more recent examples and said, "My credit report." After the car was repossessed, it all went to crap.

I finally made it to the "big guy," the owner of the truck dealership. He sat behind a big desk, wearing a massive diamond ring, and looked down on me as he shuffled my paperwork in front of him. The one thing I saw was a copy of my credit report, and I got really nervous.

"Do you consider yourself a success at this point in your life?" he asked.

I shook my head, "No, you have the report right there."

He nodded and said, "Yeah, looking at your credit report, I can see why. I wouldn't think I was a success either if I were you. What do you do for a living now?"

"I have been a comedian for the past fifteen years."

"So, what kind of comedy do you do? What kind of stuff do you talk about?"

Not really sure where he was going with it, I told him a little about my comedy being about family and parenting.

"Can you give me an example?"

Well, I thought, *I've never done comedy with just one person in an office before, but . . . okay.* I shared a couple of examples from my comedy routine, not really as I would perform it but just sort of telling him what I would say on stage.

"You're not even funny," he declared bluntly as he stared down at me. "Why did you wait so long to get out of comedy? I don't hire losers," he added as he stood and nodded toward the door. "Have a nice day."

That was a confidence builder right there, let me tell you. But I wasn't going to quit.

I had recently read that Domino's pizza had given some guys who had started delivering pizzas their own franchises. If you were on the ball and showed promise, Domino's would get you your own business. For once, I was going to have a plan. The plan was to deliver and show them how ambitious I was and get me a Domino's franchise. As I write this, I'm laughing at how ridiculous the idea was.

So I went in and applied at the local Domino's. A pimple-faced nineteen-year-old manager reviewed my application and, with a straight face, asked me, "How does what you do as a comedian qualify you to deliver pizzas?"

"It's not like you guys are splitting atoms back there, right?" I said. *What?!*

"I have an entire lifetime of experience in finding addresses in towns I don't live in," I continued. "Imagine how good I could be at finding addresses in the town where I do live!"

Pimples looked confused, so I tried again. "Every time I go anywhere for a gig, I have to find an address," I explained. "I have to find the right addresses for the comedy clubs, or I don't work. What other qualifications do I need to deliver pizzas?"

Talk about a humbling experience. Here I was, a forty-year-old man with a mortgage, a wife, and two kids, who had fallen so low that even Domino's wouldn't hire me.

I felt virtually unemployable. So I went to a temp agency and asked them to find me something, but they didn't have much for me, either. I counted record inventory at a music store—I would rather get a root canal than do that again. They got me a temp gig working for the post office. They must have sensed my underlying rage and thought I would be a good fit for government work. What could possibly have gone wrong with me working as a postal employee? (I will leave that answer up to you.) I did seriously consider it, until I did the math. Starting at ten an hour, a forty-hour week would net me four hundred dollars before taxes. I could bring that home in less than two weeks on the road.

Then a phone call from the temp agency changed everything. They said they noticed on my resume that I was a comedian. I started to get excited, thinking they were going to get me a gig.

Then they asked, "Would you like to seat people for a comedy concert of a relatively well-known comic?"

I said, "Sure, I need the money." So I told Tami that I was going to be an usher for this particular comic. She hit the roof.

"Over my dead body," she said. "You are not seating people for that hack! For God's sake, you're a *comedian.* Stop looking around for other jobs. Your agent has convinced you that you're worthless. Fire your agent!"

She believed in me, and I can't explain in words how important that was for me. She reinforced what I already knew: I had only one skill set, and that was making people laugh.

Just Two Hurting People

After I gave up alcohol and cocaine, I turned to a new drug: golf. It's every bit as expensive as cocaine and just as addictive. On the plus side, it is legal, but it still doesn't heal the wounds festering beneath addiction.

As I struggled to pay the bills and find some meaning in life, I hit the links every chance I could get. When I was returning from a gig and the plane would start to descend into Phoenix, the anxiety would return. I just couldn't bear the thought of going home and feeling that pervasive discomfort and sense of failure, so I would go out to the driving range and just hit balls. It was my sanctuary. My new strategy became just staying away and not engaging. I did it so much that Tami grew to hate golf. In hindsight, it really wasn't any different than having a mistress. It took all my time and energy.

"You can't blame golf," I told her. "If it wasn't that, it would be something else." For some reason, that didn't seem to make her feel better.

Tami's a counter-puncher. She delivers what she gets. So if I was snotty, sarcastic, and bitter, that's what she would give right back to me.

I didn't realize at the time that if I were loving, smiling, and caring to Tami, I'd get a loving, smiling, and caring wife. But at the time, I was giving nothing but a cold shoulder, so it shouldn't have surprised me that I started getting the same in return.

The truth is Tami had no friends or any other kind of emotional support system in Phoenix. I clearly didn't do anything to make her think I liked her or even found her attractive. If I had been in her shoes, I would have been looking for a way to get back to Ohio, where she at least had family and could get rid of me.

It wasn't as if we were super mean to one another, calling each other horrible names. We were just two people who were in a lot of pain and had a lot of scars, but no idea how to go about healing any of it.

The Toys R Us Question

If you are in a marriage today full of acrimony, wait until you hit apathy. Nothing is more painful than shutting down because you feel there is no hope.

I soon learned that the most painful part of a disintegrating marriage isn't when you're fighting with one another. Don't get me wrong: that sucks. Yelling and screaming at one another isn't fun for anyone. But when you stop fighting because you just don't care enough anymore—that's when you know your marriage is on life support. And that is where Tami and I found ourselves just before Christmas in 1994.

We had driven all the way to Toys R Us to get presents for the boys without saying a single word. We just sat next to each other as if we were strangers sharing a taxi. (Actually, we probably would have talked more if we *had* been two strangers in a cab.) Finally, we pulled into the toy store parking lot and just sat there for several minutes, each of us lost in our own world, the silence so thick it felt suffocating.

Finally, Tami simply asked without turning to look my way: "Do you want to get a divorce?"

There was no emotion. She asked the question like she was asking me if I wanted fries with my Big Mac.

I didn't know what to say. I didn't exactly feel much hope for our marriage improving. I was pretty sure my life was going nowhere, and I supposed one direction would be as good as another.

I felt emotionally numb. I had fallen into a routine of just getting through every day, putting one foot in front of the other, hoping to raise my kids well enough not to end up in prison, on drugs, or dead. Plus, I didn't know how to get divorced. Even though their marriage was hardly exemplary, my parents were married for fifty years. No one in my immediate family ever got divorced; they just sort of stuck it out. No one ever said it, but we all had a general understanding that when you made that vow, "for better or for worse," divorce was out of the question.

As Tami's question echoed in the stillness between us, my mind flashed back to that baggage claim in Cleveland and her saying "I guess so" when I proposed. Now it was my turn to give an apathetic answer: "I guess so, if that's what you want."

That's how unintentional we were about making these life altering-decisions—marriage on one side and divorce on the other. Our culture may tell us that neither one really makes that much of a difference—that we can take or leave a marriage without serious consequences—but I knew better. Divorce would mean big changes for all of us—good, bad, or indifferent. But in that moment, I just didn't care anymore.

Or so I told myself.

My World-Class Gift

When we returned to the house, we discussed what to do next. "How do you want to do this?" Tami asked.

"Well, we have nothing, so we don't need lawyers," I replied with a shrug. (Eventually, we went to a paralegal and paid to have divorce papers prepared.)

"I do everything else around this house," she declared, "so why don't you fill out the papers?"

I may not be good at a lot of things, but I have a singular gift for procrastination. At that, I am world-class. I have thank-you cards from 1988 I haven't mailed yet. Give me something critical to do, and I can put it off with the best of them.

Trust me, if I were a type-A, get-it-done-yesterday type of person, I'd have filled those papers out in six hours, had them notarized, and we'd have been divorced in three days.

Instead, I slowly started filling out the forms. *Names.* I could handle that one. *Address.* Again, I nailed it. But then I started scanning the rest of the items. *This seems like a lot of work,* I thought. *I could be hitting some balls at the range or taking a nap instead.* I chose the nap. I tossed the papers into a junk drawer, and there they sat for the next year and half.

Meanwhile, for all intents and purposes, Tami and I lived as if we were divorced, or at least like two polite roommates. I said I was going to get my own place—but I never had enough money, so I moved into the guest room. Occasionally Tami and I would bump into each other in the halls and say, "Excuse me," but for the most part, we stayed out of each other's way and started living separate lives. If I was reading, I'd turn my back to her while she was watching TV, and if she was reading, I'd watch TV.

From time to time, Tami would remind me to "sign the papers already," and I'd wave her away, saying, "Yeah, I'll get to it later." That had to have been confusing for the kids, who were old enough to realize something was off. We read a book on this, and basically it said most children are worried about what was going to happen to them in a divorce. So when we sat the kids down and told them we were getting a divorce, Aaron asked what was going to happen to him and Ryan. I told them they would stay in the house with Mom, and I would get my own place. Aaron said matter-of-factly, "Okay," and turned to watch television. Ryan suggested I set up a tent in the back-yard and live there.

Never Again

That's not to say the apathy never broke out into something more acrimonious. One night after our Toys R Us moment stands out. I don't recall what it was, but Tami said something that really upset me, and I stormed out of the room. She followed me, and things just escalated from there. I think I smashed a cabinet and broke some dishes. I was losing it. All the anger I had pretended wasn't there just started pouring out of me.

When I saw what I'd done, the shame kicked in. That only caused me to spiral deeper into despair, and that fueled even more anger. I had to get out of there—I was suffocating.

I walked out on to our back patio and saw the fifty-pound punching bag that hung on the porch. I used it to vent frustration sometimes, and tonight it would feel a lot of frustration from me. Years later, Tami told me every time I went out and hit that bag in anger, she thought I was hitting her. *Oh, my.* Nothing could have been further from the truth. I was just hitting at nothing, just hitting and venting.

That night, I started pounding it.

Thud.

"Aaaarghh!"

I hit it hard, and repeatedly. Over and over and over and over and over and over, again and again.

The bag flew from its mount out into the yard. I chased it onto the lawn and kicked it repeatedly. Then I picked it up and threw it against the cinder-block wall that was our fence. I did that so many times that I cracked the mortar, and the fence was about to crash.

The bag fell to the ground, but I didn't let it go. I picked it up and hurled it with all my might across the yard. By then, I was so exhausted I could barely move. The whole time I was doing this I was yelling at the heavens, "Why? Why? Why?"

I picked up the bag again and threw it as far as I could. "*Why?!*" Again. And again. "Why am I like this?!"

I finally lay there in the yard like a child, heaving and panting. I was a sweaty, exhausted mess, staring up into that starry sky. I laid there for a while, not sure what to do, but it felt like something had finally clicked within me. I just wasn't sure what it was.

The whole time, Tami and the kids were standing at the door. I staggered to my feet and walked back to the house.

Ryan walked right up to me and put his arms around me. I picked him up, and he said, "Daddy, sometimes you scare me."

I said, "I scare myself sometimes. But I'm okay now, son."

But Tami wasn't feeling calm, that was for sure. "Get out!" She yelled. "Go to a hotel; that's where you live most of the time anyway."

"Tami, it'll never happen again," I told her sheepishly. That was all I could think to say, and I believed it.

"That's bullsh*t!" She was counterpunching now—and frankly, I didn't blame her.

"Tami, have I ever said that to you before?"

She said, "What difference does that make?"

"I never said that to you because my father said that over and over to my mother. My brother said it to his wife again and again, too, and it always happened again."

I paused to catch my breath. "But I've never said it to you before because I knew it would be a lie. I didn't want to be that husband, who said 'never again' only to have it happen again and again. I don't know what happened just now, Tami, but I'm telling you that what you just saw will never happen again."

I could tell she didn't believe me—but she didn't make me go to a hotel that night. Somehow, I could sense that something deep beneath all the frustration and rage had begun to change within me. I just didn't know what that might mean. Something was happening at a subconscious level.

CHAPTER 7

Back to the Baggage Claim

One thing about the comedy world is how small it really is. Word about comedians travels pretty fast. I started hearing about a comic named Phil who wasn't like everyone else. He was wealthy and a little older than most of us.

I first heard about Phil from a good friend who worked with him—but that friend told me more about Phil's connections with golf courses than about his comedy. I thought Phil might be able to get me on Augusta National, the Holy Grail of golf.

Sometime in the early 1990s, Phil and I got together for the first time at a comedy club in Tampa, Florida—and as I expected, our mutual love of golf bonded us immediately. So we hit the links on our second day there.

The golf course is a great place to get to know someone. You are out there for four hours or more, and you only are hitting golf shots for less than one of those hours—which means you have three or more hours to just talk. Phil and I talked about a lot of different things, most of which were normal guy topics—sports, a little bit of politics, and eventually it got to personal stuff. He had watched my show the night before, so he picked up on the fact that the marriage wasn't perfect. He asked if that was true or just part of the act. I told him my marriage was headed toward divorce and gave him a little of my side of the story. It was uncomfortable, so I changed the subject and asked, "What's your story?" It's not every day that a millionaire starts a career in comedy that late in life.

Phil talked about his wife, Carol, and their three children, and that he'd graduated from Oklahoma University with a degree in architecture. Outside of designing his beautiful home in Dallas, he'd never really used that degree. He was an entrepreneur who had just sold his home security business to foreign investors and was between projects, so his focus at that time was building a comedy theater in Pigeon Forge, Tennessee. *Perfect,* I thought, *most comedians I know are like me, financially illiterate, but here is a man who knows how to make money.* I looked at my friendship with Phil as a learning opportunity. I naïvely thought if I could make enough money, I could buy the right things for Tami and fix our marriage.

Phil's interest lay elsewhere, of course. Being new to standup comedy, he was asking questions about how I structured jokes and stories, segues, etc. At one point he said, "Why do you work dirty? You don't have to, you're a clever guy." I told him, "I would rather be an accountant than do clean comedy." I couldn't think of a more boring job than accounting. (No offense to accountants reading this; all my troubles over the years with the IRS have given me a newfound respect for what they do.)

Changing the subject again, I asked how someone accumulates a lot of wealth. Phil said matter-of-factly, "You don't want a lot of money."

"I don't?" I asked, obviously a little confused. *Who doesn't want a lot of money?*

He said that I couldn't handle what little I had, so to have more would be a bigger burden and cause more problems than it solved. It would just put me in a larger and more insurmountable hole than I was in already. He then told me that he could give me one tip that would really help me out financially: "Never buy anything on credit that depreciates in value. That should eliminate 98 percent of your money problems."

Again, I was perplexed.

Then he said something that piqued my interest. He told me about a parable, the moral of which was: "When you can handle a little, you will be trusted to handle a lot."

"Honestly," he said, "you can't begin to enjoy the creation until you have a relationship with the One who created it."

That sounded New-Agey to me. I said, "Cool, where did you read that? I'll buy the book."

He said, "It's in the Bible."

I thought, *How odd.*

Phil shared more things that I found different and thought-provoking. I kept asking, "Where did you read that?" And he kept saying it was in the Bible.

I finally had enough. "Stop it with the Bible! Who reads the Bible?"

He said he did, daily.

"Isn't that a little archaic?" I replied. "*God?* God's Word? C'mon, really?" I gave him that look, like *You can't be that stupid, right?*

He said, "Let's back up then, maybe I can help you out. What's in the Bible that you don't think is true?"

"Honestly, I never read it," I said. "I am atheist. Don't really believe in God."

He said, "Then you're not really an atheist, you're a moron."

Anyone who suffers from an anger problem knows what happened to me in that moment: The hair on the back of my neck stood up and I thought I might snap. But if I did, I might lose access to Augusta National. If it was possible for an atheist to have an ethical quandary, I was in one. All I could muster in response was, "How so?"

"The Bible is the most influential book in the history of the world," Phil said. "The entire Western civilization is built on the foundation of this book, and you can't even be bothered to crack it open? That is intellectually lazy and moronic. At least read it, study it, and then make a conclusion about its veracity. You want to circumvent the hard work and just make conclusions based on nothing."

I am sure I looked confused.

"Let me give you the short answer, Jeff," he continued. "In order to discount and eliminate an infinite being in an infinite universe, you yourself have to have infinite knowledge of the entire universe. That is omniscience, and that is exactly what you are denying exists. It's an absolute negative, and you can't defend that."

"What the heck does that mean?" was all I could say.

"I say this out of love Jeff, you are not smart enough to be an atheist. None of us are."

I wasn't smart enough to figure out if he was insulting me or not. So I said, "You don't know, either."

He told me he felt he did, and if I opened my mind a crack—just a crack—that the God of the Bible could flood through and open up a whole new way to look at the world.

He then went on to tell me that he attended a church in Denton, Texas, pastored by a man named Tommy Nelson. All Tommy did from the pulpit was teach the Bible. Then Phil asked, "Would you be interested in studying the Bible? Denton Bible Church has a tape ministry that I'd be willing to sign you up for."

"Would it cost me anything?"

"No."

"Well, knock yourself out, I don't care."

He asked if I had a Bible, knowing that most households have one but never open it. I said I'd never bothered to get one. He asked if it was alright to send me one.

We parted that week as friends. To this day, I have no idea why he would have been my friend. I was a foul-mouthed, angry, bitter cynic.

After that, we generally talked over the phone, but also met up several times in person. The conversation usually progressed from pleasantries to family to Phil asking some pretty personal questions about my perspective on things. As I would complain about life and how I saw things, Phil would ask questions: *Why do you think that is? What makes you say that? How does that affect your role as a dad, husband, comedian?* Despite years of reading books by every expert I could find, I didn't have any of the answers; Phil got me thinking about life in a way I hadn't before. I didn't know it at the time, but this is how Jesus taught His followers. He got people to open up by asking questions. Phil's questions at times made me feel uncomfortable, and yet he seemed to genuinely care about how I felt and what I had to say. By the way he lived his life, Phil made me want to be a better man.

One time, I told him I want to change the way my kids saw me. I did not want my sons to grow up to become like me. I wanted to raise moral children who were mature enough to avoid the pitfalls I found myself trapped in. I'll never forget Phil's response because it really troubled me: He looked me in the eye and asked, "How do you plan to raise a moral child without some kind of moral authority?"

I said, "You just teach them the right way to live."

He said, "Which way is that, and by whose authority would you tell them that was the right way to live?" Another hard question. *Sheesh.*

When Phil gave me a Bible, I accepted it because I liked him and appreciated our growing friendship. But I didn't open it. Instead, I tossed it into the junk drawer, on top of the unsigned divorce papers. Here I was reading Ayn Rand and looking everywhere for some sort of meaning, but nothing resonated in my soul. Yet I still refused to open the Bible because I just knew that was the *one* place I would never find answers.

Phil was the only man in my life I had these kinds of conversations with. He sent me those tapes he'd mentioned but never asked if I listened to them. He never said, "I sent you a Bible. Are you reading it?" Instead, we had our talks, and they always ended the same way: "How are you and Tami doing?"

I would say, "Not too good, Phil. I am trying, but it might be too late."

He would say, "Just know Carol and I are praying for you and Tami."

That meant nothing to me at the time.

Increasingly Awkward

Around that time, another friend asked me, "Do you still love your wife?"

"Yeah, I love her," I answered honestly.

"Well, fight for her!" he insisted. "There isn't a woman on the planet who doesn't want to be fought for."

"What do I do?"

"I don't know," he answered, "but just fight for your life."

Thanks, I thought. But at least I knew that in spite of everything, I now felt there was something worth fighting for. I just didn't know how to go about it.

Tami and I continued our awkward living arrangement. I was sleeping in the guest room, and again I reiterate we were cordial with one another. Something about giving up allowed us to just be ourselves.

One weekend, she came home with an older woman and told me the lady would be staying with us for a little while until she got things figured out.

"Where did she come from?" I asked.

"She was at the dog show with a black eye," Tami explained. "She denied it was from a man, but I knew better, and I told her she wasn't going back to him. She said she had nowhere to go."

I asked the obvious question: "Where is she going to sleep?"

"In the guest room."

"Then where am I going to sleep?"

"You can come back into our room with me."

Shortly afterward, we were lying in bed with our backs to each other, and I realized that this was happening often. I put my hand on her to turn her toward me, and she said, "Quit."

"You can't even look at me?"

She said, "It is too painful."

How did we get here? I asked myself for the millionth time. *Holy cow.* It was only going to get more awkward before getting better.

The funny thing about living with someone for years is that you develop a rhythm. When something throws that rhythm off, it doesn't feel right, even if you can't put your finger on it.

Something was happening, I could feel it in my gut. Tami answered phone calls in the kitchen and then would take the phone into the bedroom and whisper behind closed doors. I would answer calls, only to hear someone hang up on the other end. I was beginning to ask myself what once had been unimaginable to me: *Was Tami seeing someone?*

When I shared my suspicions with Dick D., my sponsor, he told me, "You don't want to know."

"Really?! Why not?"

"No, you just don't want to," he assured me, "and besides, I thought you two were getting a divorce." Granted, we hadn't signed the papers yet, so I thought the basic rules of marriage still applied. We were living under the same roof. I couldn't understand why he thought I didn't want to know what she was doing.

"Well, if she is seeing someone," he told me, "don't come whining to me about it with your hat in hand. Sometimes you need to just let it go and move on."

I disagreed. "I need to know."

The Trip

The next weekend, Tami had planned to visit a girlfriend in California. I dropped her off at the airport, but for some reason, on the way home, I just kept feeling that something wasn't right. I had a bad feeling about her trip, but I dismissed it as paranoia and went home to watch the kids.

When I woke up the next day, I couldn't shake the feeling that something wasn't right. I called her friend and asked to speak to my wife.

"She's out shopping right now. She'll be back in a couple of hours."

I hung up and immediately thought it odd that Tami would go all the way to California to visit a friend and then go shopping by herself for a couple of hours. The more I thought about it, the more absurd it sounded.

So, on a whim, I called American Express and asked if my credit card was being used somewhere. It turned out it was being used to pay for a hotel room in Southern California. Without thinking, I asked for the hotel's phone number and dialed it.

As the phone started to ring, I thought about what my friend had said a few weeks earlier and asked myself again, *Do I really want to know?*

I was about to hang up when the desk clerk answered. When I explained my concern about the room charge, she offered to connect me to the room for which the card had been used. "Sure," I said, again without thinking of what I would say if someone answered the phone.

And then Tami did.

After a long pause, all I could think to say was, "Gotcha."

Silence. So, I kept talking. It was a brief conversation.

"It's bad enough you are doing this, but you want me to pay for it, too?" I could feel my rage kicking in. I felt humiliated and embarrassed and . . . emotions I couldn't even identify. "Just get your ass home now!" I did not want to go through all of it on the phone, so I hung up on her.

I immediately started pacing the house like a caged cat. There was no way I was going to put up with this. I couldn't wait for Tami to get home so we could duke it out. Finally, after all our years together, I wasn't the bad guy! She was the one who hurt me! *Ooh . . . there is going to be hell to pay for this,* I thought as I stormed around the house, slamming the door of every room I entered.

About an hour later, her friend called to tell me Tami couldn't make it home that night because she was "devastated." *What? I* thought. She *is devastated? What about* me? *I'm the one who's been hurt here!*

Her friend said Tami was booked on an 8:00 a.m. flight the next morning. "Fine!" I yelled into the phone before slamming it down.

All I've Got Left

Had Tami come home that night, I know that, as angry as I was, I would have said things that would change both our lives for the worse—and forever. Our marriage might have been on life support for a long time, but my words would have pulled the plug for good. I had no relationship with my Creator, but I can tell you I was about to wrestle with something that I now identify as the Holy Spirit of God.

It began with restlessness. As you can probably imagine, I couldn't sleep. My mind kept returning to the hotel and then running down endless rabbit trails, then looping back around to the phone call and how angry it all made me feel. I got up and paced back and forth through the house, saying out loud all the things I wanted to say—no, scream—at Tami. I was feeling sorry for myself, as if I was the only victim here. Combine that self-pity with rage and blend in a little self-righteousness and you have a pretty pathetic cocktail. Another cocktail in my life that was poisoning me, only this was one was destroying my soul.

But something was happening, something odd. Try as I might, I just couldn't stay angry.

Now, as you've probably figured out, anger is the one emotion I was always really in touch with. All the other emotions would come and go, but anger was my constant companion.

But that night was different. Every time I tried to muster up the right amount of self-righteous anger by shouting the epithet, "How could she?!" a little voice inside would remind me of some past sin of mine.

You went out partying on your honeymoon and left her alone at that seedy motel.

I'd shake that memory off and focus on the pain I felt when Tami answered the phone . . . only to recall making my pregnant wife sleep on the floor for months so I could keep buying cocaine and booze.

I was determined to get angry, though, so I really dialed in my thoughts about how she could dare to hurt me like that . . . and then remembered the night I nearly beat her to get her to leave me and took my rage out on our son instead.

Time and again, I would try to get righteously angry because I was finally "right" in this situation and *she* was wrong. Time and again, that stupid little voice would shut me down with another memory of the kind of husband I had been. Then the memory of that little old lady from the AA meeting resurfaced, poking me and suggesting that maybe *I* was the problem in my marriage. And I remembered some of the things I had said to Tami on many occasions when the rage got the best of me: "If you hadn't been pregnant, I would never have married you." Or, "I'm about as sexually attracted to you as to my sister."

Wow, I thought, *Tami has been married to a total asshole!*

I always read that when a person is dying, right before he expires, his life will flash before his eyes. I did not know it at the time, but that part of my life was dying.

But I was going to be reborn.

Those twenty-four hours saved our marriage. That odd sense of calmness—the one I had felt after throwing that heavy punching bag around the house several months earlier—returned. I didn't know what it meant, nor could I fully explain it, but I felt it. And to be honest, it freaked me out.

Needless to say, I was exhausted by the time Tami's flight arrived the next morning. And once again, I met her at the baggage claim.

This time, when I saw her walking toward me, her eyes swollen from the tears she had been crying, I was overwhelmed with a sense of how sad it all was. I could feel my heart breaking as I looked at her. All I could do was walk over and put my arms around her. I kissed her lightly on the cheek and whispered, "I'm sorry."

She flinched and pulled back a bit in surprise. I could tell she had been expecting something more—probably an angry spectacle right there in the baggage claim, where I would go off on her and throw the luggage everywhere.

But after that night of seeing myself for who I really was, I just couldn't bring myself to see her as the bad guy in this situation. I thought about listing all the reasons right then and there for why I was sorry, but that "I'm sorry" was all I could muster.

"That's it?" she asked, looking at me a little suspiciously.

"That's all I've got left," I confessed. "I'm exhausted. If this other guy is who you want, I won't stand in your way. If you want to stay married to me, we can get through this, but only if we each take fifty percent of the blame for where we are. We are a mess, those children at home need parents. So, I will own my fifty percent and you own the other fifty percent. If we get to fifty-one and forty-nine, the blame game will kill us." I paused and reached for her bag. "I, for one, am tired of fighting."

Tami told me later that she was shocked at how calm I was. She also told me she didn't feel like she had a real relationship with the other guy. Not really. She just wanted to feel loved and appreciated. He said and did all the things that I never would.

That day, however, we rode home from the airport in silence.

"Let's Go Home"

In the meantime, we soon defaulted, unfortunately, to the "status quo." Eventually, Tami persuaded me to finally finish filling out those divorce papers. So I opened the junk drawer, pushed aside the Bible that Phil had given me, and pulled them out. We then had the documents notarized.

All that remained was to file them at the courthouse, and our marriage would be over.

When the filing day arrived, we climbed into the car with the same apathetic attitudes that had led us to that pivotal moment. As we drove down the road, it was as if I could feel every bump along the way reminding me of every bump in our marriage. Bump after bump flashed through my mind as we made our way to the end.

No matter what I tried, life only seemed to get worse. The happy ending I had somehow expected to come true had turned out to be a lie. Were we there yet? Was there even a *there* there? By then, I was pretty sure there wasn't. After all those years of trying to push aside current realities so I could get to that phase of life where I had it all figured out . . . I had nothing. At that moment, I never felt further from the dream of being a happy, normal, decent man.

Suddenly, Tami said, "Pull over." I honestly thought she was going to be sick.

"This just isn't right," she said simply. "Let's go home."

Someone told me later that every man has to get "downwind" from himself—get a whiff of the aroma that comes off of him—to find out what kind of husband, father, or citizen he is to his fellow man. Well, I had gotten a good whiff of the man I was, and I knew it wasn't great.

So while we were parked on the shoulder of the road that day, I told Tami, "You're out."

She asked what I meant. I told her she deserved better than me; I loved her, but I believed I was damaged, like all the men in my family. She had given me the better part of seven years by that point, and if we filed those papers, she could be free to find someone who was better than me.

She repeated, "This is wrong. Let's go home."

I just stared at her for a few minutes, letting what she said sink in. But then I pushed her for clarity. I was tired of living our married lives like roommates.

"If we go home now, Tami, that means you are in for the long haul. When we got married, you didn't know me. I didn't know you," I said. "Now we know what we are. We know what we're getting if we turn around now. So, if we go home, divorce is off the table, and this is a renewal of our marital covenant. This won't be about just whether we are going to get through life together, but how are we going to thrive together? Are you sure you want that? I mean, this is your out, right here, right now. But if you stay, I don't want to hear a few months from now that we've made a mistake."

I reached for Tami's hand and held it. She didn't pull it away as she had at times in the past. "I'm trying, sweetheart. I am trying my damnedest to be a better man. Please hang in there, and it'll get better."

To this day, I don't understand all the reasons she suddenly changed her mind. I'm not sure even she totally understands them. But I'm glad she told me to pull over, because one of us was about to have an encounter with the Living God.

CHAPTER 8

The "Meaningless" Revelation

Despite my best efforts, the marriage wasn't really improving. It felt like more of the same. So, when Tami said she was taking the kids to Ohio for the summer, I just assumed she wouldn't be coming back. I half-expected to get divorce papers in the mail from her at some point. She told me later that even her parents assumed she had come home to stay.

But God had other plans.

Before she left, Tami told me I needed to do something about all the envelopes with cassette tapes that had been coming from Denton Bible Church. I had them scattered all over the house. Tami was tired of it, so she gathered them all up and dumped them in a pile on the living room floor so I had to walk around them to do anything.

"Will you do something about these?" she half-asked, half-insisted. "I don't care if you listen to them or throw them out. Just make them go away."

"Sure, yeah." I waved her away. I had no intention of listening to the tapes, but my gift of procrastination kicked in again.

Being in the house alone really weighed on me. I would sit in the family room and stare at the ceiling, thinking. I couldn't get away from my thoughts.

I remembered all the arguments, all the rage, and all the moments when my life felt out of control. The guilt and shame of who I had become washed over me. Everywhere I turned, a new memory came back. As I passed the bathroom, I recalled a time I had collapsed into the fetal position, just sobbing. Aaron had walked in and asked, "Why are you so sad, Daddy?"

"What a great question," I told him. I didn't know, but I was going to find out.

The philosophy books and Eastern religions I had studied were all interesting. In hindsight, they never captured the reality of the toughness of life. I was looking for inner freedom and peace in the midst of the tough stuff, but Buddha was too perfect, Plato too pessimistic, Islam too controlling, and YouTube and TikTok hadn't been invented yet. They all left me lacking. I needed something real. Something tangible. Something that actually worked in real life.

AA had been incredible for overcoming my addictions, but my heart stayed the same. I still lacked intimacy in relationships and had no sense of who I was apart from the things I did. I still struggled with rage and deep sadness about everything in my life. I was told that all I needed was a Higher Power. I would ask what that was, and they would say it's whatever you want it to be. But if I am making up a Deity, that makes me delusional. How is that supposed to work in real life? I mean, in the midst of a storm—the loss of a job, the death of a child, cancer—how do you pray to something you know you made up?

Either God existed or He didn't. I knew ultimately *that* was the answer I was looking for.

Just Push Play

I moped around for a couple of days without touching any of the tapes. But one day as I walked by the pile, I heard that little voice inside my head whisper, *Open one.*

I dismissed it. I went to grab a bite of food. *Open one,* it said again.

Alright. I started to walk towards the tapes, and another voice said, *There is nothing in there for you, it is just biblical crap.*

I was perplexed.

I grabbed a random envelope and ripped it open. There were two tapes there, both titled "Ecclesiastes." I'd never heard of it. Didn't even know how to pronounce it. My only knowledge of the Bible at that point in my life was "John 3:16" on signs at football games (you remember the guy with the rainbow hair?). But of course, I had never bothered to look up the verse, so I had no idea what that was all about.

But Ecclesiastes? That was different. I shoved one of the cassettes into the player. (For younger readers, a short explanation may be necessary: Unlike digital recordings or YouTube videos, I couldn't just scrub it to see what it was about or jump to different sections to speed it up. I had to listen to it straight through to get that information, so I did.)

It was a recording of Phil's pastor, Tommy Nelson, from Denton Bible Church in Texas preaching the first sermon in a series on the book of Ecclesiastes in the Bible. After a few introductory statements, he started to read from it directly:

"The words of the Teacher, son of David, king in Jerusalem: 'Meaningless! Meaningless!' says the Teacher. 'Utterly meaningless! Everything is meaningless.'"

Remember how I told you an alcoholic always vividly remembers his first drink? I don't know if it's true that a new believer always remembers the moment God turned his heart on to His Word, but that's how that moment was for me.

What?! That can't be in the Bible! I rewound the tape and played it again to make sure I'd heard that right.

"Utterly meaningless! Everything is meaningless."

I was dumbstruck.

YES!!! That is exactly what I thought. Honestly, I didn't know what to expect outside of my preconceived notions of the Bible and church—that it was probably all BS. But that opening statement hit me right between the eyes because I knew in my heart what Tommy Nelson had just said was true!

I leaned forward, listening intently as he read the rest of the chapter:

What do people gain from all their labors
at which they toil under the sun?
Generations come and generations go,
but the earth remains forever.
The sun rises and the sun sets,
and hurries back to where it rises.
The wind blows to the south
and turns to the north;
round and round it goes,
ever returning on its course.
All streams flow into the sea,
yet the sea is never full.

To the place the streams come from,
there they return again.
All things are wearisome,
more than one can say.
The eye never has enough of seeing,
nor the ear its fill of hearing.
What has been will be again,
what has been done will be done again;
there is nothing new under the sun.
Is there anything of which one can say,
"Look! This is something new"?
It was here already, long ago;
it was here before our time.
No one remembers the former generations,
and even those yet to come
will not be remembered
by those who follow them. (Ecclesiastes 1:3–11)

Unbelievable. Solomon really got it, and this was what—three thousand years ago? "What do people gain from all their labors at which they toil under the sun?" *Nothing*, I thought.

The eyes never get enough of seeing, the ears enough of hearing. I was staring at our video library of movies and our shelf full of music CDs—hundreds of visual and audio distractions—and thinking, *How did he know this?*

Nelson continued through the first chapter as it asked why generations pass without anyone noticing, why people forget you after you die, why we labor yet lack any real feeling of accomplishment. It was just like Mark Twain said: "At your funeral, people will lament you for an hour, and then forget you for a lifetime." *It's all meaningless!* I wanted to scream. *Yes!*

This was the ultimate tease. If you stopped reading there, you were basically left with nihilism: "Life sucks and then you die." *Really?*

No, Tommy said, you had to read on. I was ready. I couldn't have expressed it then, but my heart was lit up and my mind was opening more than a crack. If this part of the Bible was true, maybe there was truth in the rest of it, too.

Beginning to Make Sense

I popped the second tape into the player. The sermon delved into the second chapter of Ecclesiastes, in which Solomon details trying everything he could think of to produce happiness and shake the pervasive feeling of meaninglessness. His conclusion?

> I denied myself nothing my eyes desired;
> I refused my heart no pleasure.
> My heart took delight in all my labor,
> and this was the reward for all my toil.
> Yet when I surveyed all that my hands had done
> and what I had toiled to achieve,
> everything was meaningless, a chasing after the wind;
> nothing was gained under the sun. (Ecclesiastes 2:10–11)

Nelson concluded by saying if happiness were an act of human will, we'd all be happy. That made a lot of sense to me, because I had looked everywhere I could think for happiness and tried really hard to "be a better man"—all without success.

Addicts lack the simple ability to affirm ourselves because we know better than almost anyone that we are broken people. We know the anger we feel inside and all the things we hide from public view. The real disease of this life is isolation; we quietly go through our lives alone. We can be surrounded by people and still be isolated, trapped by our own thoughts and the lies we tell ourselves. *If they knew me, they would run, no one knows what I am going through, I hate myself, I am a piece of crap* . . . ad infinitum. The dialogue is endless, so we look for some semblance of sanity, something that we can cling to—a life raft of some sort. As humans, we all seek affirmation, but in all the wrong places. We look for happiness and fulfillment every-where under the sun except with God. If I could have simply affirmed myself, I would have been the happiest, most content, peaceful person in the history of the world! Lord knows I tried.

But I could not, despite what all the self-help books told me.

I was told all I had to do was to look in the mirror and tell myself what I wanted to hear, and all would be alright. The problem was, I couldn't look myself in the eye. I knew what kind of man I was. No amount of New Age pap was going to change that. But now I was con-necting to a part of myself I never had before. It was exhilarating.

I went to the junk drawer that had housed those divorce papers for so long and took out the Bible Phil had given me. For the first time, I sat down and opened it. I found Ecclesiastes and began reading the words I had heard on the tapes. There it was in black and white: *Meaningless!*

I sat there for hours, looking between the words on the page and the notes I had scribbled on a pad as I listened to Tommy Nelson preach. I began making notes in the margins of the Bible as I read, too. It was an incredible experience.

I had read plenty of decent books over the years, but this one was *changing me*—and I couldn't get enough of it. I got to the end of Ecclesiastes and read:

> Here is the conclusion of the matter: Fear God and keep
> his commandments. (Ecclesiastes 12:14)

What I got out of that very first sermon was something I have taken with me every day since then: "Life without God will have no meaning. Without meaning in your life, there is no purpose, and without purpose—suicide." Harsh, yes, but truth cannot be denied without some serious consequences. You can deny the truth of gravity, but I wouldn't walk off the roof of a twenty-story building.

I fully realized that apart from God, life had no meaning—but with Him, I could live a meaningful life.

Like the first time I took a drink and chased that feeling for years only to come up empty, I was now going to chase God daily. I somehow knew in my heart this was a worthy pursuit. At one point I wanted to run out onto my lawn, hold up this book, and yell, "Has anyone read this thing? Holy cow, what a book!"

I made a point to underline those verses and simply said, "I'm in." This was the life raft I had been looking for.

Ch-Ch-Ch-Changes

For the next month, I listened to several of those tapes a day. With Tami and the kids gone, I had nothing but time. Sometimes I listened in the car, steering with my legs and making notes in the Bible while accidentally running people off the road. (I almost met Jesus before I met Jesus!) People were still friendly, waving at me with one finger at a time. I didn't care; I was energized. At times, I found myself just sitting in my car in the driveway, listening intently, with a notepad to jot down my thoughts.

Romans was another book that really resonated with me and got all marked up in my Bible. I vividly remember reading Romans 6:21 for the first time: "What benefit did you reap at that time from the things you are now ashamed of?" (NIV). In other words, Paul was telling people to look at their past from the present point of view and re-evaluate it objectively. I wrote one word next to that: "Wow." I definitely knew I had plenty of regrets. There was no joy in remembering those moments: the drugs, the alcohol, the rage, any of it. How did some holy guy writing thousands of years ago know that feeling?

Another verse that stood out was also written by Paul.

> We also glory in tribulations, knowing that tribulation produces perseverance; and perseverance, character; and character, hope. Now hope does not disappoint, because the love of God has been poured out in our hearts by the Holy Spirit who was given to us. (Romans 5:3–5 NKJV)

Now this was a new twist on the disappointment of life. Glory? *What?* As I engaged with that verse, I looked at my life, thinking, *I have plenty of disappointment. But this is telling me there's hope for that!* Was it really possible to have hope that things would change, that maybe I wasn't locked into my current situation? *How did that happen?*

The words in the middle were things I had never valued in my own life: "perseverance" and "character." Doesn't perseverance mean you're going through something terrible? Nobody wants that, yet terrible things seemed unavoidable no matter how hard I tried.

I thought of Phil. He certainly epitomized the word *character* for me. Maybe this verse explained why he had hope. Maybe I could also find a hope that would never fall flat or let me down. I had nearly lost hope that such a thing even existed.

I kept running into verses that hit me right between the eyes. The Bible rang true to my life experience and years of searching. Not only did the writers understand the reality of life, they offered solutions that seemed to make more sense than all the other self-help books I'd read. *If this is true, and that is true . . . what else does this book know?* I began to place confidence in the words: this book knew what it was talking about. It was coming to life for me in real time; I was able to lay a part of my life over every verse I read. It was oddly relatable. It was as if scripture was actually breathing a new life into me.

As I look back on it now, I think of the story of Job (found in a Bible book of the same name). God allowed him to lose nearly everything before giving him peace. I think God did the same thing with me. I had to hit bottom and even bounce off it a few times to truly see how much I needed Him. God had to take me to that place where I was broken, weary, and exhausted to discover that I had no answers apart from Him, because that was the only way I would listen.

At the Cross

When I started listening to the tapes on the New Testament, I started hearing about Jesus. Not the Jesus I had envisioned, who made people self-righteous and pious and holier-than-thou, but a Lamb who went to the slaughter and sacrificed Himself—for me.

Tommy Nelson shared a story on those tapes I'll never forget. He had preached at a prison at one point and told those hardcore inmates, "I wouldn't walk across this stage to tell you about my religion of Christianity. But I would crawl on my knees to Hell and back through broken glass to tell you about the love of the Savior, Who went to the cross for you. He loves you just as you are. You don't have to change first. Just come as you are to that cross. Jesus loves you just as you are."

Two stories about Jesus really drove that point home for me. I loved reading stories about Jesus and the stories that He told, called parables. The metaphorical, poetic parts of the Bible resonated with me more than anything because I work at that level. Comedy is about finding stories specific to you that almost anyone can relate to. Stories can make people laugh but then help them think about life in general.

The first parable I encountered was about the prodigal son. As Luke 15 shares, this kid basically spits in his father's eye, wishes he were dead, and takes all his money to waste at a casino ("wild living" says the NIV). Then when the money is all gone, he decides to slink back home to Dad. But contrary to every expectation, the father doesn't say, "I told you so," deliver a lecture, or put him on a repayment plan. He runs toward him with open arms and throws a party because he's so glad his son has returned. (If you've never read the story, you really need to look it up right now. It's incredible.) I struggled to imagine that kind of love. To hear of a father who would accept his son after all of that—here was the Bible making me cry again.

The way Jesus interacted with people always surprised me. This was no wavy-haired, salon-styled Jesus. He showed respect and care for the outsiders, in the process making the inside crowd mad as fire. John 4 records Jesus talking with a Samaritan woman at a well. She was coming to draw water, and Jesus asked her for a drink. She said to him, "You are a Jew." Jews did not associate with Samaritans.

Jesus answered her, "If you knew the gift of God and who it is that asks you for a drink, you would have asked him and he would have given you living water." (John 4:10)

Confused, the woman responded, "But you have nothing to draw this water out."

Jesus answered, "Everyone who drinks this water will be thirsty again, but whoever drinks the water I give them will never thirst." (John 4:13–14)

I stopped right there. *This is what I've been looking for! Something to satiate a deeper part of me. This is a promise made by Jesus Himself.* All those books I'd read would wet my lips but never quenched my thirst. They weren't a waste of time; they were necessary for me to get to that moment in life, to know exactly what I was looking for. Before that, I couldn't put into words what I was missing. It was a spiritual thirst I was looking to quench, not an intellectual one, and apart from Jesus, I now knew that I would never satisfy that parched part of my soul that needed quenching. The only way I can describe how I felt in that moment is to imagine being in a desert on your last legs from dehydration, and out of nowhere someone appears with a gallon of water. That is how elated I was when I read this verse.

Holy cow, is it possible to never be confused again about life? Will this living water that Jesus gives me answer all those deeper questions of meaning and purpose? Only time would answer that, but I was ready to drink from His wellspring. He offered this gift to anyone who asked, including the Samaritan woman.

She was already despised because of her nationality and apparently had a sketchy sexual history on top of that. But Jesus talked to her anyway; He knew all about her and still thought her worth His time. He shared a message of hope with her—hope found in Himself. Then He used her, of all people, to carry His message to others. She was one of the first witnesses who told other people about Jesus.

If even these people were welcomed by God, I thought, *is it possible He would welcome me, too?*

The stories and parables of Jesus really opened up how the Bible could apply to *me.* The Bible did even more than explain the meaning of life: it showed me what grace looks and feels like. Jesus would not condemn people for the life they had lived in the past, but He would change them and use them for a higher purpose. In fact, the people who seemed to hold a special place in His heart were the people like me—broken. He knew their hearts, and when they confessed their sin and accepted the truth, He welcomed them with open arms. It was really that simple. For a newbie to the Bible, these stories were easy to digest and understand.

Genesis 2:24 says a man should leave his father and mother and together "they shall become one flesh" (ESV). This verse cut me to the core. I couldn't think of a better way to describe what Tami and I were going through; it was as if our flesh was literally tearing apart.

I kept listening, and as I did, I heard the verse that broke me. It was Genesis 1:1: "In the beginning, God created the heavens and the earth." At that moment, I knew there was a God. Why would He want me?!

All of it led to a moment when I didn't know what to do. So I called Phil. In a panic I started screaming, "There is a God, *there's a God!*"

"Yeah, I know. I have been trying to tell you for over a year," he said. "You got a problem with that?"

"Yeah, how about blasphemy, cursing Him, mocking Him, and denying His existence? Why would He want me?"

"Have you gotten to the cross yet?"

"The cross?"

"Oh, I can't ruin the ending for you," Phil said, and laughed. "Jeff, this is the Good News. It's why Jesus went to the cross and endured what He did—for the very reasons you just described. Do you think you are the first human being to trash Him? You probably won't understand this all right now, but the cross was there for you. John 3:16 says, 'God so loved the world, He gave his only Son. . . .'" (*So that is what the rainbow-haired guy with the sign in the stadiums at all those football games had been telling the world. Hmm, it all makes sense now.*)

I started crying as I told Phil what was happening to me. I was overjoyed when I heard how excited he was. I told him I had a show in Arlington, Texas, coming up and would love to get together.

Coming to Life

I wanted to tell people everywhere I went, "This book is amazing!" It was like the first time I met Tami and knew she was different than anyone else I had ever met.

If you ask me what I love about Tami, I could give you the tangibles—beautiful, smart, wicked sense of humor, great mom, loving, caring. You might say, "You can find those traits in another woman; what makes her special to you?" It was all the intangible stuff that the five senses can't discern. It was all of our lived experiences that bonded us in a way that no one else could possibly understand. This relationship I was beginning with Jesus was just like that. I couldn't explain it; I just knew it was different.

Blaise Pascal was right when he said, "There is a God-shaped vacuum in the heart of every [person] which cannot be filled by any created thing, but only by God the Creator, made known through Jesus Christ."

I couldn't get enough of God's truth, but I knew I had a long way to grow. I believe the Holy Spirit came to me the night I hit that heavy bag and that unfamiliar sense of calmness came over me. Now He was making Scripture come to life.

On My Knees

Somehow, I convinced Tami to let the kids stay with me for a few weeks that summer. I drove up to Ohio to get them. Tami stayed behind, working with dogs, while I took the kids out on the road with me to different states where I had comedy gigs. I played the tapes while we drove to share what I was learning with them.

Near the end of that summer, I took them on an extended trip to Texas, where I'd be working for a couple of weeks, so we could spend time together before they headed back to school.

Phil lived in that area also, so I was able to connect with him in person for the first time since our call. He asked if I wanted to go to church on Sunday and meet Tommy Nelson, the pastor. I had listened to dozens of his tapes by then, and I couldn't wait to meet him; I was a total fanboy.

I took the kids with me to church, and afterward, we ended up at Phil's house. He asked, "When I met you, you were searching. Do you think you have found what you were looking for?"

I told him I'd listened to all the tapes he'd sent me, as well as more about my "meaningless" revelation. "If Jesus isn't who He claimed to be, then Solomon was right about suicide," I said. "So, what am I supposed to do with that knowledge?"

"Can you admit you are a sinner?" he asked me seriously.

"Let's not go overboard, Phil," I said jokingly. (When God convicts a man, that is the easy part: I knew what kind of man I was, and *sinful* barely scratched the surface.)

So right then and there, I got on my knees and prayed:

"I'm Yours, God. I have pretty much failed at everything that defines a man. I cannot be happy on my own. Apart from You, there is no point. I know it. I've been trying for years. I need You. Forgive me."

Just like that, it was finished. It was August 17. I was saved. And there was no going back.

A couple of years later, I was at Phil's house again and saw a jar full of jellybeans. When I went to grab a handful of them, he screamed, "Don't touch those! Those are all answered prayers. You and Tami are in there."

Pretty cool, huh?

I Was There

When the world breaks a man, it just leaves him on the trash heap with all the other broken souls. The streets are full of these kinds of people. But when God breaks a man, He doesn't abandon him. He starts to rebuild that man in His image, and it's a beautiful thing. He breaks us so He can build us up again to know true peace and fulfillment.

When I got it, the change was dramatic. The very next morning, as I sat in my bed at the hotel listening to the kids watching cartoons in the other room, I thought, *Gosh, I feel so good. Different.* I was light, almost carefree. *What's going on?*

Then it hit me. The day before, I had given my life to Christ. I wondered if that was it. *Is this what I have been searching for my whole life? Am I finally* there? My circumstances weren't very different from the day before, but something had changed.

As I sat there on the side of the bed, I envisioned myself standing on a cliff overlooking a field in the valley below, as if I were looking back on my own dark life path. And I heard a voice saying, *I was there.* As I reflected on my journey, I could see that throughout my life, God had opened doors, guided, and directed me, even when I didn't recognize Him—or even hated Him. He would intervene in ways that I know saved my life.

For example, once during my early years of comedy, before I met Tami, I had been partying and drinking at a bar where three bikers were sitting. For whatever reason, they didn't seem to connect to my charm, and I just started calling them names and really ticking them off. I have no idea why I did it, but they just sat there grinning at me until I stood up to leave. Then all three of them followed me out of the bar.

As I walked down the sidewalk, even in my drunken stupor, I realized they were coming after me. I started walking faster but knew I couldn't outrun them. Just then, a police car turned the corner right in front of me. I waved my open beer can at him to flag him down. It worked. He turned on his flashing lights, pulled up, and stepped out.

"What are you doing?" he asked incredulously. I didn't even care if he arrested me for the open container at that point.

"Those three guys are going to hurt me bad," I stammered.

He stepped between us. "No, they're not. You guys go back to the bar."

The biggest of the guys pointed at me and said, "You have no idea how lucky you are."

As I remembered that incident, I heard that voice again. *I was there.*

Another time on the south side of Chicago, a friend and I had gotten drunk after one of my shows. We staggered to a train platform in a sketchy neighborhood in the middle of the night to wait for a ride. We were cutting up and acting like idiots when six or seven "yoots" (to quote the judge from *My Cousin Vinny*) moved toward us from out of the shadows. This was not a good thing.

They circled us like a wolf pack, taunting us. Then one of them looked at my friend and said, "You a comedian?"

"I am," he squeaked.

"I was at your show Wednesday night," the "yoot" replied. "You a funny mother****er. What are you doing here?"

"We are lost," my friend replied.

Those young men then became our guardians until the next train arrived! When we got on it and headed home, I asked my friend how many people had been at his show Wednesday night. He said maybe fifteen. This, in a city of three million!

What were the odds? I thought. I heard the voice a little louder now: *I was there.*

When my abusive behavior drove my wife into another man's arms: *I was there.*

When she inexplicably pulled the car over on our way to the courthouse: *I was there.*

As I thought about all the different turns my life had taken, I became amazed and overwhelmed. God had cared for me all along and used all those little details to bring me to the end of myself so I could meet Him. He was waiting for me the whole time. Jesus says to all, "knock, and it will be opened to you" (Matthew 7:7 ESV). What a beautiful image of the living God standing on the other side of a door, just waiting for you to answer His knock.

I don't mean to freak anybody out by saying I heard a voice. That hasn't happened often to me, believe me. I'm about as big a cynic as they come. But that day, it was crystal clear that God had allowed me to see my life from a new perspective.

He was there. And will be there. Always.

CHAPTER 9

Born Again

Life went on, but I knew it would be different now. In fact, it was about to change big time.

I was still concerned Tami might stay in Ohio. Her parents certainly didn't want her to leave. But she ended up coming home because she didn't want to stay with them, and it was time for the kids to get back to school.

I was happy to have them all home but was filled with trepidation at the thought of what Tami might say when I told her what had happened to me. At that point, her opinion of Christians was that they were hypocrites who praised God on Sunday but beat the snot out of you and called you names on Monday. I had no idea how she would react, but I knew I had to tell her because I was taking the kids to church.

It took me about a week to get the words out.

"I'm a born-again Christian," I told her.

"What does *that* mean?" she asked.

"That is a great question," I said with a laugh. "I really have no idea; I heard it at church on the road once. I'll tell you what I was told: I'm to love you as Jesus loves the Church—and I guess you're going to have to figure out if that's a bad thing for you and the kids."

She just stared at me blankly for what seemed like the rest of the afternoon. "I don't even know what that means," she finally told me.

"It means He gave His life for the Church, and I am to give my life for you. I am to sacrifice for you," I explained, sincerely hoping I was getting it all right.

She laughed. I didn't blame her. If you've read this far, I don't think you blame her, either. She rolled her eyes and said, "That's great, Jeff."

We had one discussion on Heaven and Hell and that was it.

"So if we die in a car crash tomorrow," she said, "the kids and I go to Hell, right?"

Wow, where did that come from?

"Look, babe, Heaven and Hell are not really my domain, let's leave that to God," I told her honestly. "I'm really not wise enough or big enough to answer that question. I've just been studying the Bible, and I believe Jesus is who He claimed to be. This is my journey. You don't have to go to church if you don't want. I'll take the kids with me."

I am sure she thought this was just one more phase that would pass. We didn't talk about my new faith again until about two weeks later. Apparently, she had seen enough of a difference in me to want to see for herself what this faith thing was all about.

She asked if she could come with me to church. She had only one rule: the preacher couldn't talk about Hell. She didn't want to hear that if we didn't do things right, then we were going to burn for eternity. That was simple enough. Since no church we attended seemed to be concerned with that part of the faith, we were free to seek a church home.

The next Sunday, she just took it all in as we sat through the service. As she recalls, she was "pleasantly surprised" that she wasn't repelled by what she saw and heard. She was even impressed that the people at the church remembered our names and seemed to genuinely care about us.

At the first church we called home, the pastor preached sermons based on the *Peanuts* Sunday cartoon. He would see a dilemma that Charlie Brown was going through and teach us a moral message based on that. In hindsight, it fed us and met us right where we were spiritually. And the pastor remembered our names the next week when he greeted us at the door. (How did the *Cheers* theme song go? "Sometimes you want to go where everybody knows your name"? Pretty cool, huh?)

Each day, I kept striving to be a better husband and father. I prayed for my kids and hoped to be a good influence on them. We started praying at dinner. One night I asked my oldest, who was around nine, to give thanks for our dinner. He said his prayer and concluded with "Amen," pronouncing it with a long "A."

"That's not how pastor says it," his younger brother argued. "He says, 'Amen'" (with a short A).

They began to argue. Back and forth: Ay-men, no, ah-men, nuh-uh, Pastor says Ay-men. At one point, Tami turned to me and said, "Are you going to say something?"

"You're not enjoying this?" I said, laughing. "I love a good theological debate. Boys, I believe you just stumbled upon the reason there are over five thousand Christian denominations in the world. Aaron, you could pastor the church of the 'Ay-mens' and Ryan, you could pastor a church of the 'Ah-mens,' then spend the rest of your natural lives bickering about who heard the true voice of God, missing the whole point of your relationship with Jesus and the fruits that come with that."

Quite proud of myself, I beamed at Tami, who said, "They are nine and six years old. How about something a little more age-appropriate, like, 'Shut up! You guys are giving me heartburn!'"

Laughter erupted around the table. Joy was returning to our house.

Some things that stood out during this period would mean nothing to anyone but us. Like the time our car broke down, which happened fairly regularly, and we were left stranded on the side of the road. I felt Tami begin to tense up. This was normally when I would lose it and begin one of my self-pitying tirades. But this time, I sat there for a minute, then turned to my oldest in the back seat and said, "I saw a gas station a mile or two back. Want to walk with me? We will get a tow truck."

Tami looked at me, "That's it?"

"I don't know why, but it just hit me: mechanics pray, too."

This was not exactly a road-to-Damascus revelation, but it was just as powerful in our lives. Scripture laid over our actual lives began to breathe into us. The one where Jesus said, "But the Advocate, the Holy Spirit, whom the Father will send in my name, will teach you all things and will remind you of everything I have said to you" (John 14:26) came to me as I was walking. I looked at the heavens and said, "Really amazing." It wouldn't be the last time that verse would come to me.

Ryan became our little evangelist. While I was driving one day, he asked me if I had accepted Jesus Christ as my Lord and Savior, and I told him, "As a matter of fact, I have."

"When?"

"August."

"I did in June," he said.

"Well, aren't you the seasoned Christian?" I said, and smiled.

He then went on to tell me that he and Miss Falcone prayed for his mommy and daddy. She was a neighbor who had come to us months earlier and asked us if we would mind if our sons attended her at-home Bible study for the neighbor children. We told her no problem; it got the boys out of our hair for a Saturday morning. The fact that she prayed with those children for their parents is a huge thing. Ryan seeing those prayers answered became something he could put in his memory bank for the hard times that were sure to come to him. I never got a chance to thank Miss Falcone for her prayers; I don't even know if she knows they were answered, as she and her family moved away before I had the chance to tell her what had happened.

I prayed every day for my marriage, too. My prayers were simple: "Teach me how to love and be loved." I was falling in love with Tami—strange, since we had been married for about eight years by that time. Understand that the problems in our lives didn't go away, but the lens through which I viewed them sure did.

Our marriage continued to grow stronger as Tami saw me living out my faith and leading by example—and how much it was changing every aspect of my life.

My comedy routine began to change as well. I stopped joking about my bad marriage and making Tami out to be the villain of the story, and changed my content and tone. Though I used some of the same stories, I rephrased them to fit my new perspective on our marriage—one that found humor in family life without seeking to degrade my wife. The new content reflected the new me much better and was no longer a point of strife in our relationship. It felt much better to tell stories that weren't aimed at tearing my wife down. I believe people picked up on the fact that I loved her. I can honestly say the anger was gone. Back when I had first started in comedy, I actually loved performing. Now I felt like I was starting all over again and having the time of my life.

Bankrupt in Arizona

As I mentioned earlier, the industry was struggling, so I was already struggling financially in comedy. By this time, in addition to not paying taxes in a while, we had fallen a few months behind on our mortgage. Staring foreclosure in the face, we decided to sell our house in Arizona and cut our losses. We listed it for only a little more than we had paid for it because we just needed to unload the albatross hanging around our necks.

With that rock-bottom asking price, it sold incredibly fast. We were excited to make a few thousand dollars—but we were literally signing the closing papers when the lady from the escrow company told us the IRS was taking what little money we made on the sale.

I slid my keys across the desk and said, "Everything I own is on that key chain, they can have it all. The only thing of value in my life is sitting at this table."

I had that sense of peace again, and just knew God was going to see us through whatever we had to face. And, for the first time in years, I was confident we'd do it as a family.

My lack of anger about the whole situation really made an impression on Tami. She told me a couple of years later that was the moment she finally believed me when I said that our family was the only thing that mattered. Perhaps for the first time in our marriage, she believed our family was my priority.

All of it reflected the changes in my inner self. Again, I went to the verse where Jesus said not to worry about this life, because He would send a new counselor in the form of the Holy Spirit to help. And He did. Despite all the financial concerns, somehow, with our new relationship with Christ, I knew we were going to be okay, because my love for my family was finally rooted first in Jesus's love for us.

Declaring bankruptcy and selling our house left us homeless for a few months as we tried to find something that could work. The kids still had a few weeks left in school, so we packed up and moved back to Ohio, staying with Tami's parents and enrolling the kids in school there to finish out the year. I had no idea how life was going to work out, but I was finally at peace, totally trusting *God* to take care of everything.

It seemed like a lot of doors were available to us in Nashville and that God was nudging us in that direction. So we moved to Nashville, and we haven't budged since. Strange how before that, we naïvely thought that if we moved, everything would be better—geographical cures, they're called. Truth is, until our hearts changed, no place on Earth would have been good. Now, our hearts have changed, and we have been at the same address for twenty-five years, as of this writing. Granted, we have remodeled the house twice, but we have not moved. I even plan on being buried in my backyard, like Elvis.

Since surrendering my life to Him, God has taken me to places I never could have dreamed of going—not only in my marriage and family, but in my career as well. It has been nothing short of amazing to watch Him lead.

For several months after we moved to Nashville, it felt like God was closing and opening doors for us every week, directing our every move as only He could do. Instead of feeling as if we were on our own and hoping it would somehow work out, I had a growing confidence that God was up to something with us. I came to call these moments "God things," and our list of them just kept growing.

Everything we needed seemed to be right there in Tennessee. I wanted to refocus my comedy in the Christian marketplace, which had a heavy presence in Nashville. Plus, Tami was closer to family now and could stay better connected with them. Opportunities just kept presenting themselves. We saw God's care and continued provision for us even in the midst of the financial difficulties we still faced.

CHAPTER 10

A New Beginning

The first time I went to my accountant to do my taxes, he said, "Congratulations! You qualify for the poverty tax credit."

"What is that?" I asked. He said we were living in poverty and for that, we got a tax break.

"*Poverty*? Really? Who says so?" He told me the federal government said so. *Cool . . . I think.*

On my way home, I called Tami on our cell phone from the front seat of one of our two cars. She answered the phone in the three-bedroom home we were renting, where she was watching one of our two televisions.

"Did you know we were impoverished?" I asked.

"Who told you that?" she said. Honestly, I can say I didn't feel very poor. As a matter of fact, Aaron had asked me once if we were poor. I corrected him and said, "No, we are broke." Apparently, I had been misinformed.

There was a time when Tami and I really were flat broke. I'm talking *zero* money to pay the bills, and nothing in the cupboard except saltines, peanut butter, and a box of mac and cheese.

But strangely enough, I wasn't panicking. A few years earlier, I would have been slamming doors and yelling at my sons for no reason or brooding in front of the television, but now I had peace even with an empty checking account. We knew God would provide. We didn't know how, but our job was to pray and trust while He did His part.

Not long after that, Tami also came home with a smile on her face.

"Guess what I have?" She said it with an impish grin, so I knew I had no chance of guessing. And I didn't really feel like playing the guessing game while we were still bouncing off the bottom of our bank account. Without a word, she handed me a check made out to her—for five thousand dollars.

"Are you kidding me?" I asked. It was nothing short of manna from heaven.

Well, not actually Heaven—it was Atlanta, and it was Tami's canine expertise that brought in the money. One of her wealthy friends wanted to put a Boxer back on the winner's list at the Westminster Kennel Dog Show. He intended to start a corporation and hired Tami as a consultant.

Then I signed with a manager in Nashville. I had known Lenny Sisselman longer than I had known Tami. He had run a Nashville club where I performed twice a year, and we played a lot of golf together. He had witnessed me at my worst, even remembering how I would go up on stage with dried blood around my nostrils from the cocaine. When Tami and I got to Nashville in 1997, Lenny noticed the profound changes in me.

Shortly afterward, he left the club to pursue artist management, and my new management company hired him. Without even thinking about it, God had brought me a businessman to handle my business; all I had to do was tell jokes. Finally. We've now been together over twenty-five years. Tami calls Lenny my other wife.

Too many things aligned that never would have if God had not been orchestrating them. Over and over, all I could say was, "Thank You, God, thank You."

All the promises I kept reading in Scripture were coming true, being affirmed as reality in our lives. "Do not worry about your life," Jesus said, and then He got specific: "What you will eat or drink; or about your body, what you will wear" (Matthew 6:25). Was He reading our minds?

> Is not life more than food, and the body more than clothes?
> Look at the birds of the air; they do not sow or reap or store
> away in barns, and yet your heavenly Father feeds them. Are
> you not much more valuable than they? Can any one of you
> by worrying add a single hour to your life? (Matthew 6:25–27)

Jesus continues His Sermon on the Mount to describe how God takes care of the flowers and the trees. Everything in creation trusts in His provision, and that meant I could, too. The more I saw Him provide, the less I worried, and the more faithful my prayer life became. "Just show me what I need to do, God, because I have to pay these bills one way or another."

We were learning to refocus our lives to "seek first his kingdom and his righteousness, and all these things will be given to you as well" (Matthew 6:33). We certainly knew from our years of misery that "each day has enough trouble of its own."

Let Them See the Light

Not only were the "God things" showing up in my career, but the difference Christ was making in my character also was drawing people's attention to me and opening more doors. I was getting invited to some of the biggest comedy festivals in the world—the Montreal Just for Laughs Festival and HBO's Aspen Comedy Festival, to name a couple. (Name a famous comedian, and I guarantee you that at some point they performed at those two festivals.) From those showcases, I picked up an agent in Los Angeles who "shopped" me around LA, looking for a development deal. From that, I was invited to a showcase of about two dozen comedians at the famous Improv club in Melrose, performing for studio execs who were looking for talent to possibly develop into a sitcom.

Every top comedian has done these, from Tim Allen to Roseanne Barr. They are not pleasant for the performer, if for no other reason than that the audience really doesn't want to be there. Most of those execs were forced to attend by their bosses.

I did the show and flew back to Nashville. A few weeks later, I got a call saying I had a meeting with a studio head, which is a rare opportunity. But I tried to downplay it when Lenny and I walked into the man's office in LA.

"So, I'm just curious," I asked nonchalantly, "why am I here?"

"I was at that showcase you did at the Improv the other night," he said. "But I don't even remember if you were funny or not."

"I know I wasn't," I replied. "That's why I'm curious." In fact, I had bombed.

"I don't remember what number you were," the chief stated. "All I remember is that you were the only one smiling. I asked my assistant, 'Remember when comedians used to be relatively happy? What happened to that?'"

I didn't even have a show idea to pitch at that point, but that meeting turned into my first development deal. It really stood out to me that this studio head could see a difference in me—not just in my jokes, but in the person I had become. Thanks to my relationship with Christ, I actually enjoyed my comedy—and all of life. My prayer before I go on stage, both then and now is, "Lord, let Your light shine through. Let them see not the darkness in me, but the light in You."

In the course of that development deal, Lenny and I went to different studios to pitch my idea for a sitcom about comedy in the midst of family life. At one point, we met with a guy from HBO.

"I saw your comedy years ago in New York," he told me. Then he said, "I just remember you were so angry!"

You know a guy has anger issues if *HBO* says that to him. But now a studio chief was remembering me for being happy.

Me and "My Guy"

After shopping the sitcom and not getting much traction, everything got shelved. Then Bud Paxton and the new Pax Network came along. We heard he was looking for clean, family-friendly programming, the way he remembered television when he was growing up. He was a fan of mine and reached out. I went to the up-fronts, where all the people involved with shows got to meet the advertisers and do a set. I got to introduce myself as someone who had a show coming to the Pax Network.

The sitcom was about a family dealing with big changes. I played an executive at a large firm who got downsized and had to move my family from Indianapolis to a different state. One of the funniest scenes from the pilot was when I took all of my office furniture with me to the new location. When my new boss tried to open the door, it only had about four inches of space left because my massive corporate office desk was wedged into the room. Lori Petty (*Point Break, A League of Their Own*) was cast as my wife, and we had three kids: a teenage son and daughter and a younger son. When we first got started, the producers asked if I could act, and I said, "I'm as bad as I'm ever going to be today. I'll be better tomorrow and even better next week."

There were definitely perks that came with being the star of a television show. One day during rehearsal, I thought I'd help out and get lunch for everyone. I took orders from the entire crew. When I came walking in with my arms loaded with burgers and fries, a producer came running over to me.

"Where were you?"

I gestured to the pile of food, thinking it was pretty obvious. "I went and got lunch for everybody."

"You don't *get lunch.*"

"I don't?"

"No. You don't. You have *a guy* for that."

"What guy?"

"Do you see that kid sitting over there doing nothing? That is your guy."

From then on, whenever I needed something that I was perfectly capable of getting myself, I turned to my guy. I felt the need to justify my guy's existence by asking him to get it for me.

So when Tami came to visit about three days later, I had to show off.

"You're gonna love this," I said. "Watch."

"Watch what?"

"I have a guy. He's my guy."

"You have a what?"

"A guy. Watch." I called him over and gestured to Tami. "She'd like an iced tea, unsweetened, with lemon. I'll take a Diet Coke, please, and thank you."

As he left, Tami asked, "Who's that?"

"It's *my guy*. Just watch!" After he came back with our drinks, I told her I didn't have to do anything for myself anymore except use the restroom. My guy did everything else for me.

Not soon after the pilot was in the can, Tami and I went to New York for a few days. I had to work one night, and Tami was on her own. She wanted to see a musical called *The Producers*, which was the hottest ticket on Broadway at that time. No one could get tickets—except maybe someone who has a "guy."

So, I called my lawyer in LA who worked with the show and told him, "My wife would like to see a play while we're in New York."

"Sure. Just let us know which one."

"*The Producers*."

"Oh, my Lord. Can't she see something else, like *Chicago*?"

"She'd really like to see *The Producers*," I said.

"Well, let me make a call."

Ten minutes later, he called back, "There's a ticket for your wife with the concierge to see *The Producers* tonight."

I was really beginning to like having a guy. To be candid, the whole experience felt like yin and yang to me. On one hand, it was exciting to have this amazing opportunity with its fun perks, but on the other, I was just getting my family back together. I remember a friend asking me, "Do you really want this?" Because if the show was a big hit, we would be living in a whole other world.

The shooting schedule for the show would require me to be in LA for three weeks and then have one week off, in which I would travel and do comedy. So, if we made it past the pilot and were successful, I wouldn't see much of my family. The kids were still at home then, and a schedule like that would put us right back to square one—Tami at home with the kids and me hardly ever with them. We'd have more money, but I'd be gone more than two hundred days a year.

But the pilot episode didn't test well, so the show never went any further. People felt like the premise was too sad. When I first heard the news, I wasn't as upset as I thought I would be—which is odd, since I'd dreamed of having a sitcom for years. The only thing I took from the whole experience was one of the props as a memento. I still have it. It was a big wooden boot that I begged my sitcom wife not to throw out on the show. Over the years since, I have caught my real-life wife trying to pitch it as well. Apparently, it is a tad gaudy.

But a few weeks after the pilot failed, I felt relatively depressed. It wasn't really about the recognition; I just remember telling God it would have been nice to have the money a sitcom would have brought us.

There is a saying in the twelve-step world that God will do for us what we can't do for ourselves. Honestly, if it were up to me, I would have taken the sitcom, but in the end, God knew exactly what was best for us.

A Battle for Integrity

As more opportunities opened up, God kept working on my character. In fact, where once angry profanity used to pour out of my mouth onstage, over the last twenty-five years, He has put a guard on it.

But it isn't only my language that has changed. The vitriolic way I used to deliver my material is gone. And now there's a different response to my comedy because there's a different heart delivering it. Today, when I look at the audience laughing, it is an entirely different group of people—not one wifebeater shirt among them.

My prayer life was changing at that point as well. Rather than praying for external things like money and recognition, I began to pray for internal changes in my character. Understand this: When you

ask God for things like integrity, He will certainly test you to deter-
mine if you are sincere. I can tell you I failed the first test.

When I was asked to do a comedy show for a parents' weekend
at a local school on a Friday morning, I agreed without hesitation.
Three or four days later, Lenny called.

"We've got a problem."

"What?"

He told me the good news: I had the opportunity to do three
corporate shows in a row on Tuesday, Wednesday, and Thursday in
Kansas City. They were paying big money. But he couldn't get me
back in time to do the show at the school that Friday at 7:00 a.m.

"What do you want to do?"

I called the person who had invited me to the school and explained
the situation to her. It felt just awful. But she was very understanding.
"Look, if you were my husband," she told me, "I'd tell you to take the
money. But could you help me find someone else?"

I found a singer to come to the school in my place. It wasn't the
comedy they were looking for, but at least they would have entertainment. Still, I felt awful. I lay awake for hours thinking about it.

After that experience, I called Lenny and told him we had to make
a hard-and-fast rule. Going forward, there were two ways we could
operate: We either take whichever opportunity is paying more, or let
our word be our bond.

"Our word is our bond," he said without hesitation.

"Great," I replied. "That's where my heart is at, too."

Of course, God always tests us when we make a commitment like
that. Less than a week later, Lenny called again.

"Wait till you hear this—the ESPYs called! They have a sports
awards program in Vegas and want to book you. You can go in a day
early. You get to play golf with all your sports heroes. Then you do a
show the next night at ten."

I said, "That's great!"

Lenny said, "Well, there's a problem. You're already booked to be in Oconomowoc, Wisconsin . . ." he paused, then hit me with it: ". . . for a sixth of the money."

I'm embarrassed to say how much money the ESPYs wanted to pay me. I was ready to hire a private jet if I could somehow find a way to do both. The Oconomowoc deal was a Valentine's banquet dinner on a Saturday night; they were willing to move the show from 7:00 to 5:00 central time, which was 3:00 p.m. Pacific. Maybe that could give me time to jet to Vegas after the Valentine's show? Bottom line: we really tried, but we couldn't work it out.

When we had exhausted every option, Lenny asked, "What do you want to do?" I remembered our conversation: Our word or the money? I didn't hesitate. We told the producers we couldn't do the ESPYs, and I never lost a minute of sleep over that.

This is what integrity looks like in practice: a man integrating what he believes with how he lives. Like everything else in my life, I am still taking baby steps in this area, but I am proud of what we chose that day.

That's the kind of work God is doing in me. He used these challenges to my new faith and convictions to shape, mold, and test me so I could keep getting stronger and more like Him.

Bob and Bill

One thing I have learned is that His ways are not our ways. When we tend to think something isn't possible, He is already lining up events to do it. Before Tami and I had moved to Nashville, I was there for a week-long gig at a club where I met up with an old comic friend of mine, Beth Donahue—one of the funniest human beings I have ever met. We had worked together on the road a year or so earlier. I asked her what she was up to, and she said she had gotten into morning radio in Nashville. I told her I was a born-again Christian. She laughed and said her brother Don was, too. In fact, he was part of something she called a Christian Brat Pack, which also included a friend of hers named Chaz Corzine, who was the manager for Christian music industry icon Michael W. Smith.

It turned out that Chaz was a huge comedy fan, so Beth invited him to one of my shows that week. We have been close friends since. He believed in me and did whatever he could to help me get a foothold within the faith industry. After Tami and I got settled into our home in Nashville, I started hanging out with Chaz a lot. It was fun just to be introduced to the people he knew. I have never met a more connected man than him. I always joke that you could be hunting in the forests of Montana, bump into a total stranger, tell him you are from Nashville, and he would ask if you know Chaz Corzine. As it turned out, Chaz was also Gary Chapman's manager. (That's Gary the singer, not the *Five Love Languages* author, whose work I also admire.) Gary was pretty hot back then; he had a television talk show on the Nashville Network every night called *Music City Tonight*, and Chaz asked him to put me on. I think I did the show five or six times over the course of a year. Gary was also doing a show on Sunday nights at the Ryman Auditorium and invited me to come down to watch.

In case you don't know, the Ryman Auditorium is called "the Mother Church of Country Music." It was the home to the Grand Ole Opry from the 1940s to the 1970s. Elvis Presley sang there. Minnie Pearl performed on that stage. Harry Houdini. Louis Armstrong. Helen Keller. Johnny Cash. Dolly Parton. You name the top performers from any genre, and they either performed there or it was on their bucket list. You can feel the cloud of witnesses from over the years watching when you walk through the door.

I had never been there, so I thought carefully before responding: "You're inviting me to the Ryman? Ah, let me check my schedule. *Are you kidding?* Of course, I'd love to go!"

I even got to go backstage, where I could just sense all the ghosts of Country Music Past hovering as everyone bustled to prepare for the show.

At one point, Chaz came over and asked if I wanted to do a few minutes on stage. He had asked Gary and was given the OK. Who wouldn't jump at a chance like that? So, I did a ten-minute set. Unbeknownst to me, that set would change the course of my career.

A few nights later, I got a call from someone who said he got my number from Chaz. He went on to say that he was head of the Christ Presbyterian Choir in Nashville, and they were doing a banquet for the choir at Belmont University. He had seen me at the Ryman; would I be willing to do a show at Belmont for the choir? It didn't pay anything, but because Chaz had made the intro, I said no problem; I had nothing to do that night.

But in that audience at that free show was a man who was about to change my life. His name was Bob MacKenzie.

I was hanging around afterward to chat with anyone who wanted to, and a lady came over and started what turned into a ten-minute monologue. I still don't know what it was about. What I do remember is the man standing behind her. He was smiling and just standing there listening to the woman prattle on. I thought they were together. When she finished, she walked away, but he was still standing there.

I said, "That's not your wife?"

He laughed and said, "Oh, no. Don't know who she is. Holy cow, you should have said something! I could have hurried her up."

He put his hand out to shake mine and introduced himself, "Hi, I'm Bob MacKenzie."

I said, "Nice to meet you."

He then went on to tell me how much he enjoyed the show and said I might be a fit for a singer friend of his named Bill Gaither. I said, "Who's that?"

He said, "You never heard of Bill Gaither?" I told him I never had. He then laughed and said this was going to be a lot better than he thought. He went on to tell me that Bill was a Southern Gospel singer who did various events around the country and had a small gathering of folks that get together every year in his hometown of Indianapolis. Would I be interested in meeting him?

I was thinking, *I just performed in a living room for thirty people. This Indianapolis thing has got to be bigger than that.* So I said I would love to.

Before he left, he told me he needed to get in touch with his friend but would be getting back to me. I gave him Lenny's name and number, and he left.

The very next day, Lenny called me and said, "Who did you meet last night?"

I said, "I don't know—some lady that yakked my head off."

He said, "No, it was a man named Bob."

"Oh yeah, he came up after the lady. What about it?"

Lenny said that I had a lunch appointment with a singer named Bill Gaither who apparently does an event in Indianapolis called the "Praise Gathering." I remembered what Bob had said about it being a little gathering. So we booked a lunch with Mr. Gaither. I still had no clue who Bill Gaither was, but I was about to find out. At lunch, I had to come right out and tell him that I had never heard of him before but thanked him for the opportunity. He said, "You never heard of me?"

I shook my head. He laughed and said that Bob was right—this was going to be better than he thought.

He told me he likes to work some comedy into his shows and explained what he wanted from me. He said a third of his audience would laugh at whatever I said because they were out to have a good time, and another third may not quite understand what all my jokes were about but would join the laughing group because they also wanted to have a good time. The last third is who I would be paying attention to. Those people had never been given permission to laugh their entire lives. They had been told that life on Earth is something to be endured until you get to Heaven and then you can experience joy.

Bill said, "You make these people laugh, and we will have a long relationship."

So of course, I did the show—and it turned out Bill's "little gathering" was about fifteen thousand people!

I had never worked for any crowd near that size. After I delivered my first joke and the audience responded, the hair on my neck stood up and I thought, *Whoa, I can get used to this.*

After my set, while the audience was still applauding, Bill walked over, put his arm around me, and whispered in my ear, "You got them all the way to the back wall, thank you."

I toured on and off with Bill for six or seven years. His group became a second family to me.

Getting Bill Gaither's stamp of approval at that early juncture of my new faith walk really opened up the Christian market to me. After I encountered Christ and started seeing the changes He made in my life and my work, I had been wanting to shift my audience. I'd told Lenny I wanted to speak at more churches. The problem with that is when your resume is filled with nothing but casinos and nightclubs, pastors are a little hesitant to give you their pulpit for an hour. We had only booked one church in the entire year before I met Bill. But after the Praise Gathering, pastors were a lot more relaxed about trusting me with their congregations.

Joy and the "Good Life"

I love something Socrates once said: "The unexamined life is not worth living." If we fail to examine our lives, those uninspected parts can sneak in and destroy us.

I never examined my life before I was thirty, when everything fell apart. I went through life checking the typical boxes: house, car, beautiful wife, healthy children. I discovered it's possible to check all those boxes and look like you have the perfect little American dream family from the outside but still be hollow and miserable inside. By all appearances, I was living high for a little while (literally), but eventually, my unexamined life cracked because the foundation wasn't strong. "The American dream" is not strong enough to hold the weight of our search for fulfillment.

Let me say that if a house, car, or even family is the only place where you find meaning in your life, you may wake up one day to find it's suddenly gone. Or you'll just live with terror every day that it might all fall away—because eventually, it will. It's all nothing but sticks that eventually wind up in the landfill.

If you expect another person to make you happy, that might be the most unstable foundation of all. People are fickle. Just look at yourself! Another person can never be a constant source of joy—unless you find the truly perfect Person, and He doesn't walk the surface of Planet Earth anymore.

We tend to think we can fill the holes inside ourselves with stuff, success, or acceptance; but the reality can never live up to the expectation. We are always let down, and then we start looking for the bigger house, the prettier car, a person who makes us happy all the time. But those holes are never truly filled.

Tami and I both realized that the change happened when we understood that happiness and contentment needed to come from someplace other than ourselves, our material possessions, or anything else we could manufacture. We ultimately needed to find it through the Bible and through Christ. It couldn't come from our kids, our domestic life, my comedy, or her job. Those things can make us feel "happy," but there's a difference between that superficial happiness and deep contentment.

Now, we have a good life—but not a perfect life. For example, before one show, Tami and I had an argument over the phone. I then said I had to go to work and hung up without apologizing. I felt like an ass.

But I pushed it aside, went on stage, and did my set. When it was over, I went upstairs and just sat outside the green room, feeling miserable. As I sat there, head bowed, I heard a pair of heels come down the hallway. *Click, click, click, click.* Out of the corner of my eye, I saw a woman approaching, but I didn't want to talk to anybody, so I kept my head down as if I were praying and just waited for her to walk by.

Once she passed, I finished my "prayer" and looked up—just a little too soon. The clicking stopped, and she turned to come back. When she reached me again, she stopped and looked me in the eye.

"I don't know why," she told me gently, "but God just put it on my heart to tell you that He loves you."

I broke down right there in the hallway. I looked up and said to the heavens, "Really?"

To think that the Creator of the Universe cared so much about the pain I was in that He sent another angel of mercy to me just at the right time melted me.

God knows I'm a skeptic at heart. If someone standing on a stage had said that to me, I would have immediately discounted it. But this was my experience, no one else's; I will never forget it.

I called Tami right away and asked her to forgive me.

CHAPTER 11

Against the Odds

Life is a wonderful little roller coaster. One of the AA sayings I heard for years that drove me nuts was, "This, too, shall pass." It didn't matter what I was feeling at the time—a pink cloud happiness or deep, black depression—someone would mutter, "This, too, shall pass." *Oh, shut up!* But it is true: Life never stays put.

We were getting ready for another big event—a weekend getaway with the kids on the road—when Tami made a shocking discovery. It was October, and Rosie O'Donnell had been talking on television about Breast Cancer Awareness Month and the importance of self-exams. So Tami did a self-exam in the shower and immediately felt a lump. Initially she didn't believe what she was feeling, then she doubted, worried, and told herself it was nothing—but she couldn't talk herself out of it. She finally told me about it a few days later.

At that moment, life changed for us. We scheduled a biopsy for the following Thursday.

Beginning the Journey

Tami drove home in a fog. I hadn't been with her at the appointment. The techs had been whispering after her mammogram, but the surgeon bet it wasn't cancerous. They did a needle biopsy and said they had to send it out to a lab to get tested. In reality, they looked at it in the back office and could tell from that it was abnormal. But no one called us.

Then, on an unrelated visit to her gynecologist, the doctor looking at her chart patted her on the shoulder and said, "Sorry about your breast cancer." *Whaaat?*

No one had prepared her for the news. After the doctor said the word *cancer*, Tami said everything else turned to goop in her ears, sounding like Charlie Brown's teacher. The drive home was a blur—and then she had to tell me.

Tami began thinking about the very real possibility that she could die. Both her grandmothers had died from breast cancer. The severity of the news weighed on her until a new way of thinking took hold: She realized she could step off a curb at any time and there would be no tomorrow. There just aren't any guarantees in life. It is precious and beautiful and could end for any of us in any number of ways. So, what else was there to do but get out of bed and do the next thing? She had young kids, responsibilities, and Christmas shopping to do.

Right away, Tami wanted to take drastic measures—a double mastectomy. But the doctor encouraged her to take some time to do some research and think about it. Her cancer was aggressive; the pathology was not good. She read *Dr. Susan Love's Breast Book* and came back with a dozen questions for her surgeon.

He was confident that he could get all the "margins" of her cancer, so Tami opted for a lumpectomy, then began a dreadful round of chemo right after the holidays. (Boy, was that a fun Christmas. All

Tami's siblings came over, and it felt like a funeral until she called them out on it, saying, "Stop it. I'm not dead. Start talking, everyone!")

The chemo she was given was called the Red Devil. The nurses wore hazmat suits to prepare it, complete with gloves all the way up their arms and spit shields. Then they would bring out the syringe and shoot the concoction into my wife's veins. *What could go wrong with that?* I learned that it could actually kill the veins, but the hope was that it would kill the cancer first.

We made quite a splash in the office at her first chemo treatment. A British comedian named Dame Edna was on the TV in our treatment room, so we sat there just cracking up while Tami was getting chemo. A nurse even came in and asked, "Are you guys all right?"

We wiped tears off our cheeks (not the kind she usually saw from patients) and replied, "Oh yeah, we're fine."

The nurse looked skeptical, no doubt wondering if we needed a psychological consult. "We don't normally hear a lot of laughter coming out of here."

Tami quipped, "Well, do you normally have Dame Edna on the TV?"

We needed moments like that.

Before long, locks of Tami's hair began falling out in handfuls. I would take her to a restaurant after treatments, but all her taste buds had changed. Now she hated her favorite cheesecake and couldn't step foot in a grocery store. She would stay in bed for three or four days after every treatment. We went through seven months of this and then twelve more weeks of radiation.

Our boys responded in different ways. Aaron saw Tami cutting off her hair and asked why she would do that. "You're not even sick!" he said, clearly in denial. Tough-love mom that she is, Tami made him say out loud one day when his friend came over to play: "My mom has cancer." Ryan understood, accepted it, and even accompanied us to some of Tami's radiation appointments. He decided then that he was going to become an astronaut so he could cure cancer in space. (His plans may have changed since then.)

Though it was both mentally and physically taxing, Tami was determined not to let her spirit wander into negativity or anger. She gave herself one day a week to feel sorry for herself. So, she would have pity parties in the bathtub with wine and candles, the whole nine yards. If a friend called during that time, I'd tell them, "You can't talk to her right now. She's feeling sorry for herself." I would go to the bathroom and hold the phone up so she could tell her friend, "Woe is me. I've got cancer." It was a good for a laugh.

At other times, she acted like absolutely nothing was wrong. I came home one day, and she had the cabinets all gutted. Bald from chemo, so wiped out she had to sleep most of the day, she thought it was a good time to clean out cabinets. My protective instinct had to protect her from herself. "What the heck are you doing?" I demanded.

"If I died tomorrow," she shot back, "your mother would come in here and think we live like pigs." She said she couldn't stop thinking about it for two days, so she did something about it. Who thinks of stuff like that? But that was her attitude. It was the same attitude she had at the worst part of our marriage: *Either I'm in or I'm out. And if I'm in, there are things I have to do. I have people to take care of. I have a house to keep clean and food to put on the table, and I'm not going to lay down and wallow in this garbage.* And if she wasn't going to wallow, she might as well get on with what had to be done.

In the Storm

I had asked the doctor what Tami's odds of survival were, but he said he didn't do numbers. Even if the disease had a 99 percent cure rate, Tami could be the 1 percent that didn't make it. He looked at her and asked, "Are you going to live, or are you going to die?"

"I'm going to live," Tami declared frankly, as if she had told him what she had eaten for breakfast.

"That's good," he replied with the same candor, "because there's no expiration date stamped on the bottom of your foot. I've had forty-five-year-old women come in here, get the diagnosis, and age twenty years in two months. If you get fixated on 'hurry up and live,' because you are dying, then start dying."

Tami took that as affirmation of her positive attitude and ran with the encouragement. Through it all, I knew I needed to be strong for her and our family, so I did what I could to shoulder the burden and be a listening ear when she needed me the most. But inside, I was struggling.

I was, in a word, stunned. *How could this be happening? Things were just turning around for us. Our marriage and family were finally becoming something we treasured, and now this?* As you might have guessed, that shock quickly turned to anger. *Really, God? We haven't been through enough?*

I often ask people, "Do you want to have some fun with the Lord? Ask Him to show you what He sees in your heart. Pray that for a week: *Show me my heart.* And see what He reveals to you."

When Tami was diagnosed with cancer, I saw my heart, and it wasn't pretty. I was angry—and not in a "righteous" way, either. I was angry because *my* career and life were starting to get better, and now this cancer thing was going to put a damper on it. When I finally realized how selfish I was being, it broke me.

Despite the continuing cancer battle, we experienced a sense of calm in the midst of the storm. My prayers were simple during that time. I didn't even ask for healing. I just said, "God, help us put one foot in front of the other and do what we need to do. Give us the right doctors and help us make the right decisions." For the most part, we tried just to focus on each day and the blessings it brought.

The Church Ladies

I always enjoyed working with the Gaither group. Everyone is great at what they do and passionate about doing it for the Lord. After Tami's diagnosis, I was part of the taping of another Gaither Homecoming event. Tami was three treatments into chemo and had just lost her hair. She wasn't sure she was up to being around people and worried that her health would hurt my career. Would people think I couldn't be fully present when my wife was going through something as serious as cancer? But these people were our friends, and eventually, she decided she would go and just hang back from the crowds.

Bill Gaither had said that if anyone had something on their minds during the taping, we should share it freely, because it wasn't a live show. So, as I finished my comedy set and was about to leave the stage, I felt a tug on my heart.

"Is it all right if I share something?" I asked Bill.

"Absolutely," he said, nodding.

So I told everyone about Tami's cancer diagnosis, and all that we were facing at that moment poured out of me. As I opened up, I felt a sense of relief, knowing these brothers and sisters in Christ would be there to support us.

As I finished talking, Vestal Goodman, a larger-than-life matriarch and the first Queen of Southern Gospel Music in general, stood up and asked, "Is your wife here?"

I pointed to where Tami was standing at the corner of the stage, wearing big hoop earrings so people wouldn't look at her bald head.

"Is it all right if we pray with her?"

"You'll have to ask her," I said, suddenly realizing the public scrutiny I had brought to Tami.

"Can we pray for you, Tami?" Vestal asked gently. To my surprise, Tami welcomed the request.

"Please," she said softly.

They pulled her toward me and gathered around us. Several people laid their hands on her. Bowing our heads, we stood there, united in prayer, lifting her up to the Lord. We were brand-new to this whole thing, but it was such a cool experience. We soaked it all in.

Tami later told me that at that moment, surrounded by people petitioning the Lord for her healing, she felt God's presence. A feeling of peace, love, and appreciation washed over her unlike anything she'd ever felt before.

After the event concluded, we headed to the cafeteria. As we sat down to eat, Tami leaned over to me and said with confidence, "Jesus was there. I felt Him. This isn't going to be fatal."

But not all the little old church ladies were so nice. Often, they would come over and pat Tami's hand and tell her how their friend had died a miserable, horrible death from cancer, "but I'm sure you'll be fine." Not exactly reassuring.

After one event, two sweet old ladies came to our merchandise table and asked Tami, "Now, sweetie, what sin do you think you committed against God that would bring this cancer on you?" I suppose they intended to help her repent so the cancer would go away that moment. Tami told me this much later because if I had overheard the comment, I would not have reacted in a very Christian way. Tami, of course, insisted that we give them the benefit of the doubt; they were probably well-meaning, not vicious. (Can I just say that this is how the devil can work, even with well-meaning people? It's a good lesson for all of us to remember. If you can't extend the same grace that Christ has given to us to someone going through a hard time, maybe you shouldn't say anything at all.)

The comment took her to her knees, because it resonated with something she was already wondering: *Was* God punishing her? After all, in the past she had committed one of the "big ten" sins. I believe it was number seven on the list: "Thou shalt not commit adultery." Maybe this is what she got in return. *Was God like that?*

Tami carried this lie for years, never telling me. In the meantime, she turned to the book of Job and the well-meaning friends who asked the same question: "What did you do that God is punishing you?" But the whole book shows that those friends were wrong. That is *not* what God is like.

Between Tami's upbringing and my being completely new to Christianity, it was a struggle for us not to be legalistic in moments like these. It's easy to think that God wants us to follow all the rules before He will bless us, and if we mess up, He's going to punish us instead. Finally, an older believer plainly told me, "You're denying God's grace by elevating your standard so much. You can't work yourself into Heaven, right? If that's all because of God's grace, then the rest of life is, too."

God wasn't punishing us; He actually blessed us as we walked through cancer. God gave us exactly what we needed at each point in our lives. He enabled us to handle every situation He put in front of us.

Stronger through the Storm

Cancer actually helped Tami solidify her relationship with God. She had accepted Jesus as her Savior as a little girl but had been ignoring that relationship for a long time. Being face-to-face with a disease that could take her life forced her to trust Jesus in a way she never had before. From that moment on, she had a newfound faith and a passion for serving the Lord. She began stumbling forward right alongside me, making many life changes along the way. I saw the Holy Spirit working in her life and the spiritual growth that was taking place. There's no way we would have gotten through without Him.

We learned to understand the peace that's possible to experience even in the brokenness of life. These things happen. And in the midst of that storm, we leaned on the One who loves us and gave Himself for us.

Now, don't get me wrong. It was an extremely hard summer, but with God on our side, we made it through. The trial made us stronger than ever. And just like always, He was in every single detail. Though this was not a battle we would have chosen to face, God used breast cancer as a final breakthrough to Tami. She surrendered her life to Him, and we only grew stronger in the process.

We praise God that Tami has been in remission ever since! And because of her experience and tenacious research, she's had the amazing opportunity to walk several women through their own cancer journeys, including my mother. Tami's openness and expertise through my mom's battle with ovarian cancer helped restore my estranged relationship with her. When another of Tami's friends was diagnosed with breast cancer, she talked to her on the phone every day until her treatments were done. The Apostle Paul says in 2 Corinthians 1:3–4 that we comfort others with the comfort that we have received, and that's exactly what Tami has done.

A New Hope

So many times, we blame things that have happened for the way we are today. Maybe we look back at something our parents did or said that shapes the way we now interact with our spouse, kid, or someone else. But we need to understand that whatever pain has been passed on to us can find its resolution in Christ. We don't have to be a slave to that generational cycle. We can find a new hope.

When I first committed my life to Christ, I realized how much I'd been forgiven throughout my life. As the Apostle Paul writes in Ephesians 4:32, "Be kind and compassionate to one another, forgiving each other, just as in Christ God forgave you." No one gets through life without being forgiven; you wouldn't have any long-term relationships with anyone if those people hadn't forgiven you along the way. And if *you* didn't forgive, you would cut your losses and move on, just like I did before I got married.

Forgiveness became so much easier as a Christ-follower. "Forgive as I have been forgiven" became almost a mantra with me. I had made so many mistakes, and yet they were all forgiven. I realized I needed to do the same for others. Whatever wrongs had been committed against me needed to be forgiven, and I needed to let go of grudges I was holding onto. I had to release my bitterness and resentment toward people who had wronged me, including my parents for things they had done. And I've got to tell you, it was incredibly freeing to let go and move on.

Forgiveness was the catalyst for changing my marriage. And it's really what I was seeking from Tami, even if I didn't fully understand it at the time, when I picked her up from the airport the second time and told her we each needed to take 50 percent ownership of our problems. Otherwise, we would have resented each other forever.

If I had walked into Alcoholics Anonymous thirty-five years ago and somebody had walked over, put their arm around me, smiled, and said, "You need Jesus Christ," I would have left and never come back.

If God had sat me down thirty-five years ago and said, "This is what I'm going to put you through for the next eight to ten years:

Alcoholism, bankruptcy, infidelity, nearly divorce, and cancer . . . but in the end, I'm going to introduce you to My Son, Jesus Christ," I don't know if I would have signed on.

All of this leads me to believe this is why God doesn't tell us our future ahead of time. He's God. We're not. He doesn't give us more than we can handle with His help. And I'm thankful to worship a God big enough to know me intimately, as well as the paths I needed to take to understand who He is and what He's done for me.

Fallen but Forgiven

I'm not perfect now that I've found Christ. Not at all. In fact, Tami and I sometimes joke that if I were to go on the reality show *Survivor*, it would not end well—especially if anyone knew I was Christian. After three days of low blood sugar and no sleep, I'd likely be cussing up a storm, throwing logs at everybody, and generally reflecting pretty poorly on Christ. But living as a forgiven sinner is my reality every day. Not perfect, but forgiven.

One time I shared about my continued fits of occasional anger in a church small group setting and got strange looks from the other members. The leader pulled me aside afterward and asked, "You're in AA, aren't you?" When I told him I was, he told me, "Yeah, that's probably a little too much truth for this group in a church setting." I thought that was a shame; maybe if we Christians were more candid about our shortcomings, other people might be more open to hearing about the reality of new life in Christ.

I tend to forget I have "a peace that surpasses all understanding" at the airport and the golf course. I've lost it many times on the golf course, unfortunately. One time I even broke every single iron in my bag and then tossed them in the pond after a particularly horrid round. Every. Single. One. Yet Jesus still loves me.

Another time years ago, I was traveling and grew so angry at the flight delays that I hurled my backpack against the wall right there in the airport by the gate—and my Bible came out and slid across the floor. Another traveler picked it up and handed it back to me saying, "Hey, you might want to read this." *Nice.*

I went to get a Diet Coke and cool down. When I came back, there were four police officers huddled around the gate. They all turned toward me as I walked up.

"You're probably looking for me, right?" I asked.

"Did you throw the backpack against the wall and cuss and leave, sir?"

"I threw the backpack, yes," I admitted. "But I didn't cuss."

"Then we're looking for you," one officer said, stepping closer. "Witnesses say you did cuss, sir."

"Look, I am a comedian and I make my living with my mouth, so I am very careful about what comes out of it. And I didn't cuss," I told him. For some reason, it was important to me that they knew I hadn't crossed that line when hurling my bag across the airport like a spoiled child.

We started talking and, fortunately, I started cracking jokes and got the cop laughing. Soon someone from the airline approached us and asked how he could help.

"You could get some more baggage handlers so we don't have these delays," I cracked. "It takes me longer to get my luggage than it does to fly to Detroit."

"Oh, I'm sorry, sir," he said. "I can give you twenty-five thousand award miles for your troubles."

"I don't want miles," I deadpanned, "I want baggage handlers." The officers were cracking up now and ready to let me get back to traveling.

"Oh, by the way," one said as he turned to go, "you might want to watch your behavior. We had to put you on the watchlist." *Nice.*

Jesus describes Himself as the Good Shepherd. He describes how sheep listen to their shepherd's voice: "He calls his own sheep by name and leads them out" (John 10:3–4). Our Shepherd knows every one of our personal details. Romans 8:34 tells us that He intercedes for us. If we put these two thoughts together, we see that Jesus is praying for us by name today. That's a powerful truth for someone like me, who tends to think of the bigger picture. *Well, sure, He's got the whole world in His hands. He holds the stars and gravity and controls the weather and nations. He's got all that stuff to worry about—so He's definitely too busy to worry about little ol' me down here in the middle of Tennessee.*

But in those moments of doubt, I know I'm wrong. Jesus knows every detail of what's going on inside us and in our circumstances. He calls us and prays over us by name. I can just picture Him praying for Tami by name. Praying for Jeff. Praying for you.

Meanwhile, all we have to do is listen for His voice and follow Him. When we follow His lead, it always turns out well in the end.

CHAPTER 12

Reflections on the Journey

"God invented time; man invented the watch." My life may not have changed as quickly as I would have wanted, but one thing I learned is this: We all want struggles to be over, but the mature person realizes that it is in the midst of struggle that you encounter the divine.

If you are still reading, that's a good sign. It means you are looking for something better. Your life may be even more miserable than mine was. Your story may have taken so many sharp, twisted turns that it has left you feeling dizzy and exhausted. Your marriage may be just beginning to show signs of problems, or you may feel like it is so far gone that not even God could save it. But wherever you find yourself, it's important to know two things:

First, there is hope. I'm not going to get all preachy or anything, but I have found the hope the Apostle Paul describes that is experienced in the midst of hard stuff:

> [W]e boast in the hope of the glory of God. Not only so, but
> we also glory in our sufferings, because we know that suf-
> fering produces perseverance; perseverance, character; and
> character, hope. And hope does not put us to shame, because
> God's love has been poured out into our hearts through the
> Holy Spirit, who has been given to us. (Romans 5:2–5)

Second, there is no quick fix to the struggles of life and marriage, but persevering is worth the effort. You cannot use a three-step process or wave a magic wand to resolve all the problems you will face; there's just a lot of work. But that work can produce something more beautiful than you could ever imagine.

It reminds me of a Japanese art form called *kintsugi* which restores broken pottery, not by concealing damage, but by high-lighting the repairs. When a piece of pottery breaks, the potter restores it by using lacquer mixed with precious metals. The end result is a work of art that celebrates the piece's history, including the damage it has suffered along the way. The restoration after the breakage adds to its value.

Too often in our culture, people choose a plastic approach to marriage—and just about everything else, it seems. Maybe that is why Tami always insists on only buying our grandkids real wooden toys, not plastic stuff that won't last; too many people are content with throw-away everything, including marriages, and she wanted to teach them different values.

Perhaps the real beauty of marriage comes not from the absence of conflict, but weathering storms together and seeing God reassemble our pieces in a way that creates an even more brilliant work of art. If God had sat me down before Tami and I got married and told me all that we would go through over those eight years before Christ, even if He let me know we would come to know His Son and true peace,

I don't know what I would have chosen. That's why He gives us one day at a time.

In fact, I want to be clear on this point: I now love Tami more than I ever dreamed possible, and yet we still take one day at a time. We still fight sometimes. The road still gets tough. There are days when I still stomp around like an impetuous child.

We are not there yet. None of us will ever arrive *there*, that place where we think everything will finally be working out. There is no *there* there. There is only *here*, right now, the time which we have been given to live today. And it's not going to be perfect. That's not how life in this broken world works, and it never will work like that this side of Heaven.

Are you willing to candidly examine your life? To what lengths are you willing to go to discover your purpose? I had to reach the bottom before I was open to hearing God speak into my life—and even then, there was no quick fix, just a lot of work. But it has been worth all the effort. God didn't create you to live in misery, anger, frustration, or mired in addictions. I now enjoy a happy marriage and life full of meaning, significance, and peace. And so can you.

So, as you consider my story, may I suggest you consider five questions about your own?

What defines you?
What do you value?
What are your expectations?
Which voices do you listen to?
Where is your hope?

These questions get at the heart of the lessons I've learned. I hope they can help you, because now more than ever, we need men to find meaning, purpose, and direction—to strengthen their families, to strengthen the communities, and to strengthen our nation. Let's look at each of them in turn.

What Defines You?

That's not an easy question, is it? But the answer can set the stage for the choices you make at the forks in the road of life. As I've moved from addiction into wholeness, I've noticed that what defines me has changed as well.

For a long time, comedy defined me, but it doesn't anymore. It's simply the way I earn a living—and I happen to love it. Now I am able to tell Tami that there's no pressure up on stage anymore. I just really love my job. I've waited forty years to get here. Plus, now that we aren't living gig-to-gig to make ends meet, Tami and I get the chance to travel together. For example, we took a seven-day road trip down the Pacific Coast Highway. We just relaxed and enjoyed the views, the sunshine, and the time together. We wouldn't have been able to do that even ten years ago because I would have been thinking about money, new material, and my next big gig.

Matthew 6:21 has an interesting take on what defines us: "For where your treasure is, there your heart will be also." For a long time, I didn't really understand what that meant, but I know now that wherever you spend your time and energy is where you invest your heart and soul. The one finite thing we have in this life is time; if we spend it on something frivolous, our hearts and souls will be invested in frivolity.

As you know, I have some intimate personal experience pursuing frivolity (or "vanity" as Solomon called it). Tami says I have an addictive personality, and I know what she means. I can exchange one addiction for another. When I quit cocaine and alcohol, I filled the time and obsession once reserved for those things with golf.

When I moved into golf, the search for the "high" was the same, only this time, I was hooked on everything related to golf. I used to buy *Golf Week*, *Golf Digest*, Golf Channel—you name it. I was preoccupied with learning everything I could.

I was constantly working on my swing. When I wasn't doing the motions, I was obsessing about it in my head. I was constantly thinking about my golf score. If I got a good score, I would be in a good mood. If I played terribly and got a high score, I would be in a bad mood. I was thinking about golf in my downtime and in my busy time. If I wasn't thinking about the game that I had just played, I was thinking about the game I was going to play next.

In the same way that alcohol had been a barrier to intimacy in my marriage and my relationship with myself, so was golf. I called it "time for myself," but it was really time away from obligations, responsibilities, and those who loved me.

It really got out of control. When Tami would be out of town showing dogs, I'd have a few weeks at a time to spend at the golf course. On one particular day of 95 degrees and 95 percent humidity, I walked eighteen holes, came in and had lunch, then walked another nine holes. Then I went down to the range because I wasn't hitting the ball very well. After a while I started to feel like I sort of worked it out. My hands were starting to hurt, so I started to walk to my car. But on my way, I turned back to "just hit a few more" to make sure I had it dialed in. After about five of those little trips back and forth, I realized I couldn't bring myself to leave. So, I called my son, Ryan.

"Hey kid, come get me."

"Where ya at?"

"I'm at the golf course."

"Did your car break down?"

"No. The car's working perfectly fine. I just need you to come and get me."

"What do you mean?"

I really had no good answer. "This is what addiction looks like."

That summer, Tami called me every couple of days while she was away. Every time she asked me where I was, the answer was always the same: the golf course. When she was on her way home, she called and asked again.

"Where are you?"

"Where do you think I am?"

"The golf course," she sighed, then added, "You're mentally ill. You need help."

I'm glad to say it's been a few years now since my obsession with golf ended, and I feel like I'm in a good place with that now. That experience helped me understand why it's so important to understand what defines you.

I was convinced that other people's opinions of me and the faux happiness of alcohol and drugs or golf brought me joy, but they were all roadblocks to authenticity and my true identity. When I think of all the time, money, and energy I spent on those addictions over the years, I look at it as a waste.

Buddha said your desires are what make you miserable. At one point, I thought if I could get rid of my desire to drink, to get high, to golf, or whatever, I wouldn't be miserable anymore. If I could just stop desiring these things, I would find joy. But I found that it's impossible to get rid of desires. Even the desire to get rid of desires is a desire. There's always something missing, a gap that needs to be filled.

The answer to "what defines you" sets the stage for the moments of your life, whether big or small. If your identity isn't rooted in something solid, your core values and beliefs will bend like willows in the wind—easily changed by the people around you, a bad day, or disappointing experiences.

What Do You Value?

There's always a desire for something more, so ask yourself what you desire. Pastor and writer Max Lucado talks about developing an "understanding," or discernment, within. That's the Holy Spirit. When the Holy Spirit dwells in you, as He does in all who trust in Christ, you have the voice of discernment within you. Our job is to listen to it, even—*especially*—when it goes against our own desires.

If you were to look at my history with comedy, golf, addiction, and my wife, you'd think I desired fighting, numbness, and a lack of intimacy. Now, with the Holy Spirit, I choose love over nitpicking. I choose authenticity over addiction. Certainly, I still overrule that small, still voice inside sometimes, but that "understanding" helps me choose the right path most of the time. I'm able to look at Tami now and genuinely say, "If it brings you joy, it brings me joy." Or "I don't want to go to that home or flower show, but I will because I want to be with you." I look forward to a hundred more trips down the Pacific Coast Highway with her by my side. I'm finally at a point in my life where my decisions and actions consistently, if imperfectly, mirror my values.

When I speak to men's groups, I tell them that if they spent half as much time on their marriages as they do polishing their cars or throwing themselves into playing or following sports, they would be much happier for it.

If I could share with you one practical tip that would make your life better, it would be to choose your battles more wisely. So many times, we choose pettiness over compromise and good communication. If you can't remember what the fight was about a week later, it wasn't necessary.

So, think about the biggest issues you have with the people in your life. Write them down and revisit the list in a week. I bet a lot of them won't even be issues anymore.

What Are Your Expectations?

Nearly every frustration, fight, or problem in my marriage can be traced back to an unmet expectation. In fact, I've learned to say that the misery in your life can be found in the place where reality and your expectations finally intermingle—and usually clash.

Now, expectations are normal. They are part of being human. Whenever two people enter a relationship, they bring in two different sets of expectations, hopes, dreams, and even fears. When Tami married me, she expected a loyal partner. In some ways, as she has told me, she was just hoping for someone to treat her with love and respect and get her out of her painful life circumstances. What she got was more like a part-time partner who weighed her down—an adult child instead of someone who could lead her to a better place.

When our expectations fall short of reality, we get either an explosion or an opportunity. I've chosen the explosion more times than I'm proud to admit. After meeting Christ, Tami and I started choosing the opportunity together. By God's grace, that helped restore our relationship and lay a strong foundation for our lives moving forward together.

But before we could make that pivot, we had to do the painful work of resetting our expectations. We had to face the points where our expectations were conflicting and figure out how we were going to live differently.

If you haven't reset expectations with your spouse before, prepare for some discomfort. Prepare to have your eyes opened to misalignments. Reaching honesty and healing in your relationship can require some soul surgery—without anesthesia. But finding the pain points means healing is possible.

Here are a couple of areas where expectations usually collide:

Communication
Responsibilities

Intimacy
Quality time
Alone time
Raising children

How reasonable are your expectations? How do you communicate with each other about them? Start talking about them with your spouse (and with a trained professional if necessary).

The key to this journey is to keep your heart open to "progress over perfection." (That's another phrase from AA I've found helpful in other areas of life.) We all know Rome wasn't built in a day, and neither is a solid marriage. Don't worry about reaching perfection; just keep moving forward.

For example, over the years, I would run into other men on the brink of divorce. Sometimes I'd ask about their irreconcilable differences. One of them said, "She doesn't want me doing comedy."

"What were you when you got married?" I asked.

"I was a carpenter."

So, she married a carpenter. Interesting. Then I asked, "Do you think she came in with some expectations? Did you talk to her about what going from being a carpenter to a comedian might entail?" I just wanted to get the guy thinking. Maybe if he realized that his wife's expectations weren't being met, they could start talking about that, and reconciliation would become possible.

Many couples drive wedges between themselves when they assume their spouse should be on board with whatever they want. If their spouse disagrees, he or she becomes an opponent.

My own story gave me a new hope to share: It is possible to overcome irreconcilable differences, and even infidelity. But you have to communicate about expectations. It's still hard to figure out what Tami needs from me. It helps immensely when she says exactly what she needs. The words "I would like . . ." would be magical, but I have figured out that my wife uses language a little differently than that.

For example, if she wants me to do something, she asks me a question like: "Is that your underwear on the bedroom floor?"

I could take this literally and sarcastically respond, "Well, it better be, or else I'll have a few questions of my own!" Or I could correctly translate it and respond, "Yes, and I'm sorry about that. I'll put them in the hamper right this instant." But if she says, "I need you to tell me I'm pretty," and right away I tell her, "Oh, you're beautiful," she'll say, "You're only saying that because I told you to." (Sometimes, we guys just can't win!) But her *point* is that it would be nice if I spontaneously said it from time to time. (And frankly, I do think she's gorgeous. Did you read that, Tami?)

I once heard someone say at a marriage-enrichment event: "Husbands, you need to say you love your wife. She doesn't know that." These kinds of instincts need to be honed over years and years of practice.

Where you spend your time can reveal what you value. If your expectations about how you spend your time are unclear, that is an invitation to problems, too. It's healthy to talk about expectations and recognize where they are not being met. Get those out into the open. At that point, another dangerous expectation can come into play. Often, we expect that once we communicate our needs to our partner, he or she will immediately start meeting them. *Well, I've told her what I want, and that should fix it.* That's a wrong expectation about expectations.

Too often, when expressed needs remain unmet, the response is, "Oh, well, I guess that means we can't make it work. I'll go do my own thing." But have you considered your spouse's side? What are *her* expectations? How can you compromise, adjust, and start serving her?

For example, Tami once told me, "I knew I married a comic, but I didn't realize what that meant." When I was gone every week, she had to face the reality that she had thought marriage was going to be a partnership, but it wasn't. As I said earlier, we each had to acknowledge our side and do the work of getting realigned. For me, that meant imitating Christ's sacrificial love and showing that to her.

Tami was correct: a marriage should be a partnership in which you make decisions together.

Which Voices Do You Listen To?

I once heard a great line about the voices we hear in our heads: When I hear negative information about myself, sometimes I have to stop, sit down, and ask my brain, "What is your source of information?"

I would say most, if not all, of us have negative voices speaking to us in our minds. They come from all sorts of places, including our past experiences and people who have spoken into our lives. And they keep echoing for decades. If you hear that kind of voice in your head, you're not alone and you're not a psycho (as far as I can tell); it's a normal part of growing up in a broken world.

Your voice might say, *You're a loser.* Instead of swallowing that wholesale, pause a second to ask, *Who or what is your source of information, my friend?*

And then ask yourself, *Why am I calling myself a loser today? Because I stubbed my toe on a curb while I was walking? Is that valid? And will I believe it?*

My own internal voice often tells me I'm a piece of crap. That's my anti-mantra. I once heard my father tell my mom when I was in another room, "We raised another lazy piece of sh*t." Hearing that sure didn't feel good. His words still play inside my head at times.

Finding Jesus didn't make those voices stop. Instead, I have had to do what the Apostle Paul says and "renew my mind" (Romans 12:2). I do that by regularly taking in Scripture and biblical teaching that trains my mind to think differently about myself. After all, the Psalmist says that as a human being, God made me just a little lower than the angels, and we are the prize of all His creation (Psalm 8:5). Not only am I *not* a piece of crap, He thought highly enough of me to love me and sacrifice Himself for me.

Talk about incredible value! That is who I am—and who you are. So, whatever voices may be playing in your head that portray you in a negative light, you can choose to listen to different, more positive voices that accurately reflect your true value.

It's also possible that those voices we hear are not just from our pasts. I now believe there are demonic and angelic realms that can influence our world, our thoughts, and our behavior. I'll tell you why.

Many years ago, Tami and I were attending a big event in Washington, D.C. At the time, we had a whippet, like a miniature greyhound. He was a pretty neurotic dog. The night before the event, Tami was finishing something in the kitchen after I had gone to bed. When I was nearly asleep, she came in with the dog; we all got reunited on the bed, and then Archie started whining. I thought he needed to go outside, so I got up and let him out. I brought him in, went back to bed, and was almost asleep when he started again. But he wasn't just whining; he was screaming like he was in pain. He was really howling, which was not normal for him at all. In my exhaustion and frustration, I am embarrassed to say that I beat him to make him shut up.

Tami woke up and started yelling at me, and then I lost it. I just got totally crazy. I screamed back, "I'm gonna go outside! I want to kill myself!" I started toward the door.

She called Ryan, who had become quite a big kid by then, and said, "Grab your father!"

Both of them ended up wrestling me to the ground. As I lay on the floor in front of the door, I kept repeating, "I want to die. I want to die."

"You don't want to die."

"Yes, I want to die."

After a few minutes, I was so exhausted from fighting them that I just collapsed.

And then, just like that, the anger went away. I looked up and said, "Let me up. I'm okay."

"Are you sure you're okay?" Ryan had learned a thing or two over the years of living with me.

As I got up, I told them, "I do not know what that was about."

Tami went into the kitchen; I went to the bedroom and sat on the bed. Then the voices in my head began: *What would your Christian fans think? You hypocrite! Hypocrite! Hypocrite! You're just a hypocrite!*

About five minutes later, Tami came in and asked, "So, we're not going to talk about this?"

"I can't talk about where it came from," I confessed. "I just have no idea."

We had to get up to catch a flight at four in the morning, so there was no sense in going to bed. Instead, we flipped on the television and saw Pastor Adrian Rogers talking about demonic and angelic realms and the hounds of Hell. I had always told people I wasn't a devil guy. I believed in the devil, but I was not really thinking too much of him or his power.

But Adrian got me thinking about what had just happened. It hadn't felt like me at all, but like something else was possessing my soul. It wasn't normal. I'd never done anything like that before, and I never did it again after that.

The next day, we arrived at the event—exhausted and a bit confused, but glad to be there. And wouldn't you know: the second person I met that day was none other than Adrian Rogers himself. I couldn't believe it!

So I had to ask him about what he said on television. He was serious about demonic influences and the spiritual battle we fight against them. When I told him about my experience, he reminded me of Jesus's authority over demons, and that I had to fight back in the spiritual battle.

When I start thinking about some of the times I just snapped and what took over inside me, it's hard to explain. It was not normal anger. It was something different. It seems really stupid, but if you're a golfer, you might understand. Even when I was by myself on the golf course, sometimes, if I hit a few bad shots, the anger would just start coming from nowhere. I really think that was a demonic influence trying to get a foothold in my spirit.

Some people might say, "Well, I think demons can become an excuse for bad behavior." My whole upbringing taught me to be quick to anger, and I'm not saying devils drive every fit. But at times, there has been something different about the irrationality of mine. Sometimes anger is not just coming from within; it's an attack from without. When it unites with what's already within you, it gets downright scary, especially if you don't have the Holy Spirit living in you.

I've also noticed that, when we started to get things in order in our marriage, sometimes either Tami or I would get really snippy all of a sudden. Then we'd step back and think, *What is really going on?* I believe that could be a spiritual attack. I've heard speakers like Josh McDaniels and Sean McCarron say to pay close attention to your marriage when you're trying to do something with spiritual impact, because that's when attacks tend to come.

Where Is Your Hope?

Someone once asked me, "How does an atheist from the south side of Chicago wind up living in Nashville, Tennessee, as a born-again Christian working at churches?" It could have been a great setup for a joke, but it wasn't. I was being asked how God had done that.

I went from being the most hopeless wretch the Windy City has ever produced to a guy who became a decent comedian who actually brings people joy; from Vegas casinos and Atlantic City to working churches. I have to tell you that twenty-five years ago, I never would have expected to be here.

How did I get here? Because God told me my life is meaningless without Him. Harsh, but true. But it still took years of me pulling a Samson and blindly knocking down the pillars around me to see just what I had become. Once everything collapsed, and after I tried blaming everyone but myself, the truth became obvious: I was the reason my life was all messed up.

When I crawled into my first Alcoholics Anonymous meeting so many years ago, all I wanted was to stop drinking. Was that too much to ask? My goal in life was to be sober and a civil human being to my family. But the problem wasn't my affair with Jack Daniels, but my heart. I was an angry, bitter, cynical man. I was harder on my family than anybody. I thought if I could stop drinking, then I could stop asking *Where am I?* and *Why am I not there yet?!*

AA told me to pray to God. When I said I didn't believe in Him, they said, "Then find something in this universe that's bigger than you." As broken as I was, that was the hardest thing I had heard yet. *Something bigger than me? BAHAHA.* I thought, *How is that possible?* Isn't it amazing that the human ego can be so large? My ego was so big, I should have had my own field of gravity. I couldn't get on my knees. I wouldn't pray to anything. I was going to figure it out on my own!

Today, I know the truth. And my greatest joy is being able to share what I believe with people who need to hear the truth about life. I used to hate interacting with fans after performances; I beat myself up so much before and after that my self-esteem could not handle any feedback, either positive or negative. Now that I've found peace, my favorite part is talking with people and hearing their stories and how mine has impacted them. So many people have told me how my stupid jokes got them through the isolation of COVID or helped a family member who was addicted or depressed. Lenny teases me because now I'm the last one to leave as the pastor is turning out the lights and locking the door, trying to shake one more hand, take one more picture, listen to one more story. I absolutely love hearing the stories, because making something useful out of *me* is something only God could do.

It's all a God thing, but I also have to give credit to the person God used in my life to lovingly persuade me toward this change: Phil. God does the heart work, and He usually uses a human tool who will reach out in love and open their mouth with truth. Phil was that person for me. God put exactly the right guy in my path to open my heart to the Gospel. He had everything that was attractive to me: a comedian, a golfer, someone who actually seemed content in life and wouldn't fly off the handle at all the crazy stuff I said. He took my life and my thoughts seriously and challenged me to think. He was patient even as he watched me wrestle with my dissatisfaction with life.

He never asked, "Hey, did you listen to that tape I sent you? It really would solve all your problems!" He didn't react when I told him to shut up with all the Bible talk; he knew that meant I wasn't ready. He practiced what they now call relational evangelism and discipleship, understanding that spiritual change is a process that takes months and years, not just an instant conversion. I've never met another man like him, and I hope I can be like him one day.

I believe a man is not fully alive until he has something he's willing to give up his life for. I wanted to think I'd give up my life for my kids and wife, but until I met Christ in my living room surrounded by those tapes, I proved every day what I would give up for them: nothing. I didn't give up my addictions, temper, or pride. How could I die for them when I couldn't even die to myself?

But I'll tell you what I'll give up my life for now: my Savior and my right to profess this faith. There is nothing more valuable than Him. As I have grown in my faith, my perspective has changed. The jokes I make have changed, and the ones I laugh at, too. I used to think Christians were a joke, but now I realize that I laughed at them because I was inadequate to save myself. I was doomed to fail. But God . . .

Apart from Him, I have no hope. Not only are my life and marriage no longer meaningless, but I have hope and joy today because of Him!

So, I have to ask, my friend: Where is *your* hope?

Who We Are

Who we were is not who we are

Today we choose to walk a different path

So feel free to throw at us the stones of our past

We will not deny them but use them to humble us

For today our shield is the Lord

And it is because of who He is and the blood that He shed

That we no longer have to run from our past but can embrace it and walk with peace into our future.

—Jeff Allen

Acknowledgments

Holy cow! Where do I begin? There is no book without my wife, Tami. For over a decade she pushed me to write this thing. I would tell her I am not a writer, and she would say I was—just one more thing she was right about.

My children Aaron and Ryan. You guys lived this. Thank you for not sending me the bill for what I am guessing will be countless hours of therapy.

Thank you to my friend and manager, Lenny Sisselman. I have known Lenny since 1984; he knew me when all of these things were taking place and yet he continued to call me "friend."

Also, the crew at Salem Books for believing that a cranky old comic like me had something to say.

My agent, Tim Grable from The Grable Group, for keeping me busier than I should be at my age.

I thank my friend Chaz Corzine, who knocked down doors that would have normally been closed and told people to take a chance on me when my resume was nothing but casinos and nightclubs. Shockingly, pastors were a tad hesitant to give a comedian the pulpit for an hour. He put his reputation on the line for me, and for that I will be ever grateful.

Bill Blankschaen, your patience with me knew no bounds. Thanks will never be enough.

Andy Andrews, you have no idea how important your belief in me has been; thank you for your grace and kindness. I am honored to call you friend.

Phil Glasgow, I will never know why you put up with me and my constant whining, but thank you for not bailing on me and literally loving me into the Kingdom, putting the Bible into my hands, and letting God do the rest. Thank you.

Tommy Nelson, who's teaching of the word resonated with me at the right time. Thank you, Tommy.

Bill and Gloria Gaither, who took a risk putting this curmudgeon on their stage without really knowing what I was going to say. Thank you for that; you guys literally kept a roof over our heads for years.

To my fans, who encourage me daily: thank you for your kind words and more importantly your prayers; they do not go unnoticed.

Finally, to my Lord and Savior Jesus Christ, who continues to do a work in this broken vessel. You know me better than anyone and You choose to love me despite it. Thank You.